ICEBREAKER
Third Edition

ICEBREAKER
A MANUAL FOR PUBLIC SPEAKING
Third Edition

Tom Fisher
Tracey L. Smith
Lewis and Clark Community College

WAVELAND
PRESS, INC.
Prospect Heights, Illinois

For information about this book, write or call:

Waveland Press, Inc.
P.O. Box 400
Prospect Heights, Illinois 60070
(708) 634-0081

Photo Credits

© Chicago Tribune, 1992, 139
Gordon, Brian, 16, 99
Los Angeles Times Photographic Archive, UCLA Special Collections, 6
Rowe, Neil S., 33, 42, 79, 81, 83, 99, 114, 150

Contents

1

Speech and Stage Fright

Chapter One Outline

I. Speech is relevant to most areas of your daily life.
   A. Your family relationships, as well as your careers and profession, demand speech abilities.
   B. A good speaker must size up a situation.
   C. A good speaker clarifies ideas by verbalizing.
   D. A good speaker encourages others to share ideas.
   E. Public speaking is not different from day-to-day communication.

II. Communication is a process composed of several elements. Visual Aid: The communication model will help you understand this process.
   A. The initiator of the communication is called the sender.
      1. When a thought is initially experienced, it is seen as a mental image.
      2. The next stage is choosing verbal and/or nonverbal symbols to represent that mental image.
      3. The process of turning mental images into symbols is called encoding.
   B. The encoded idea is the message.
      1. The message is what you want the other person to understand.
      2. The message travels through some media or channel.
         a. The channel may be visual.
         b. The channel may be audio.
         c. The channel may include audio and visual representation.
   C. The receiver is the person you want to understand what you are saying.
      1. The receiver must turn the symbols (encoded message) back into mental images.
      2. The process of turning symbols back into mental images is called decoding.
   D. The message sent is often not the message received.
      1. Ineffective communication may result if the encoded message is unclear.
         a. The symbols chosen to represent the sender's mental image were not understandable to the receiver, thus causing a problem.
         b. When encoding the message, information was left out and caused a misunderstanding.
      2. Messages go astray because the sender and receiver did not share environments.

a. Environments include everything there is about a person.
b. No two people share exactly the same environment.
c. If environments don't overlap in the area we are communicating about, a misunderstanding could occur.
3. Noise interferes with receiving the message.
   a. There is external noise which is sounds produced outside of your ears.
   b. There is internal noise which is thoughts and feelings we experience in our own bodies and minds.
   c. There is physical noise which refers to actual hearing problems or defects.

III. Communication involves listening as well as speaking.
   A. Hearing is the reverberation of sound waves on the ear.
   B. Listening is the willingness to understand oral communication.
      1. Our minds have time to wander.
         a. People speak at 150 w.p.m.
         b. People can assimilate 450 w.p.m.
      2. The tendency is not to pay attention unless the message is on a favorite topic.
      3. You spend lots of time listening throughout the day.
      4. You must listen to nonverbal messages.

IV. The major concern beginning speakers have is how to deal with stage fright.
   A. Your psychological makeup is probably most important.
      1. You do not fear actual physical attack.
      2. You fear appearing like a fool.
   B. Your physical reaction needs to be understood.
      1. The energy is adrenaline.
      2. This force is strong.
   C. There are easy, practical suggestions for dealing with stage fright.
      1. Use a Lifesaver to cure dry-mouth syndrome.
      2. Use deep breathing to relax your body.
      3. Use toe-tapping to expend nervous energy.
      4. Yawn to relax.
      5. Expect that the speech will go well.

V. There are three basic styles of presentations.
   A. There are impromptu speeches.
   B. There are manuscript speeches.
   C. There are extemporaneous speeches.

VI. There are three general kinds of speeches.
   A. There are informative speeches.
   B. There are persuasive speeches.
   C. There are entertaining speeches.

Chapter One

Speech and Stage Fright

Introduction

Here you are, in a speech course, *a public speaking course!* You're not sure what you've gotten yourself into and perhaps you're a little frightened. It's okay, look at the others in the class. Odds are they are thinking and feeling the same way you are. A national survey rated speaking to a group of people as the second most feared event in life. It was preceded only by dying which ranked number one in the poll. As a matter of fact, 32 percent of those responding feared public speaking more than death. All of the students in your class are in the same boat. All must give speeches and act as audience for others. You can learn a great deal from each other, giving advice and support as you all face that potentially frightening podium and beyond it those seemingly hundreds of pairs of prying, evaluating eyes. Most audiences are on your side. They want you to succeed! You won't believe that now, but keep it in mind as we get started.

Tell Your Audience How to Remember Your Name

Purpose: The purpose of this exercise is to give the novice speaker a topic they can easily talk about.

Procedure:

1. Prepare a one- to two-minute speech on how your audience can remember your name. This can be your first name, last name or your entire name. You might tell a story about how your parents named you, or what your name means. You could approach this exercise by name association, a rhyme about your name or an amusing anecdote about your name.
2. Present your speech in class.

The Importance of the Speech Skill

Whether the speech situation is one from a podium or across coffee cups, it is **communication**—the act of exchanging thoughts, feelings and ideas. To live in today's society, you need to learn how to get your messages across to all kinds of people: your spouse, your employer, your professor. How do you react in a job interview? How can you describe to your mechanic just what is wrong with your car? How can you convince your boss that you deserve that raise? How can you persuade the Parent/Teacher Organization to purchase books for the library? These are only a few instances where speech is essential.

You learn your first lessons in dealing with society through your relationships with the members of your immediate family. You learn to tell when Mom is mad and to warn your sister not to talk about the broken plate. You learn to join your father in a discussion about fixing the car and you enjoy a conversation about each other's day. You ask your five-year-old nephew about the new toy he just received for his birthday. All these situations and thousands more rely on effective communication.

As a human being, you experience a whole range of feelings, and you possess the intelligence and the vocal power to share them. Not only is your family life based on speech, but as you grow, develop and leave the family circle, your outside interests and profession will most likely demand speech abilities.

Your career may demand speech abilities.

A good speaker must be able to size up a situation (sometimes in a few seconds) and use the proper phrase which will gain him or her the desired sale, promotion or good will of his or her audience. Not only will you reap rewards from others for the ability to express yourself and listen to others, but your self-confidence will grow as you find yourself able to send and receive clear messages which satisfy your needs.

You clarify your own thinking on a subject by verbalizing your feelings about it and encourage others to participate by sharing theirs. This sharing results in a free exchange and cements personal relationships, increasing your own self-esteem and that of your partner or audience.

Take the incident of having to break a date. You have met your Prince Charming and he has finally asked you out for that first date. After you accept, you find that you already have something planned for that evening. You now are faced with the rather delicate problem of breaking the date without hurting his feelings so that he will ask you out again. You have to persuade him, using techniques which put you in the best possible light in terms of credibility, and make your audience (him) accept your line of thinking. You are not manipulating your partner; you are merely explaining your point of view with enough support to allow him to see things your way. As you gain support for your way of thinking, your confidence will grow and your ability to explain yourself in future instances will improve.

You can translate this practice of persuasion from the interpersonal exchange into the arena of public speaking: revealing to an audience some facts on an issue, tracing a line of reasoning which suggests some action on the part of your audience, and finally getting the audience to see your point. You gain the satisfaction of influencing your audience, a wonderful boost for anyone's ego.

Say you are seated in a meeting of your Parent/Teacher Organization when someone suggests that the group build a new playground spending $10,000 for the project. You believe that the money could be better spent for acquisition of more books for the library. You could sit in that meeting and mutter under your breath to your neighbor in the next seat, or you could seek recognition from the chairperson and explain your objections to the whole assembled group. Chances are that there will be others in the assembly who feel as you do, but lack the courage to be the first to stand and explain their objections. Imagine the feeling of accomplishment you will have as you realize that you are able to face opposition and overcome it in Western civilization's time-honored tradition of open debate on public issues.

Introduce Your Partner

Purpose: The purpose of this speech is two-fold. It will allow the students to get some basic information about their future audience and give experience in basic speech making. It can also be used as a beginning interview.

Procedure:

1. Pair up with one other person in your class, preferably someone you don't know.
2. Talk with this person for 20 minutes.
3. Prepare a three-minute speech of introduction about your partner. Include any information you find interesting.
4. Present your speech with your partner.

Public speaking really is not different from what you do on a day-to-day basis. Communication—efficient and effective exchange of ideas and feelings—is based on the same principles whether you are deciding what toppings to have on a shared pizza or standing behind a podium in front of an audience presenting an explanation of an audit report. Getting your ideas and viewpoints across to another person or persons requires the same skills for both situations. Perhaps an analogy will help clarify the message. Speaking to a group of friends versus speaking to an assembled "official" audience, is much like the similarities between writing a personal letter and writing a business letter. Your goal for both letters is the same: send a message, share some information. The differences occur only in the specific form that the letter takes. In an informal personal letter to a friend you might not be very concerned with sentence structure, spelling, punctuation, etc. You might refer to "inside jokes" without explaining them or use slang terms that you and your friend share. In a business letter you would be very careful of the grammar, spelling and the "proper" use of words. A discussion with friends versus a formal speech is very similar to the letter analogy. Talking with friends you might use slang, be somewhat careless about your diction and be seated. That same discussion could be presented as a formal speech, delivering the very same message, but you would carefully organize your thoughts, make sure you were speaking clearly and probably be standing behind a podium. Essentially the difference is one of form, not purpose. Consequently, the skills you learn in a public speaking class can easily be transferred to your general interpersonal communication resulting in fewer misunderstandings with clearer messages being delivered. Let's take a look at just how communication takes place whether it is in a formal or informal situation.

The Process of Communication

Before you can actually learn to communicate more effectively, and increase your speaking confidence, it is necessary to understand the elements of communication. To help make this process easier to understand, we will use a pictorial representation commonly referred to as a *communication model.*

A model is a small re-creation of another object or event that makes it easier to study and understand. Most of you have probably put together some kind of model before and you know that it represents that 1915 Ford or B-52 plane or Frankenstein's monster. We can do the same thing with the process of communication.

The first step in sending a message actually occurs when a person has an idea, opinion or feeling and wants to let another person know about it. The person who initiates or starts the communication process is called the **sender**. When we experience a thought, we do not initially think about it in words, but rather experience it as a mental image or picture. For example, let's say you want to ask

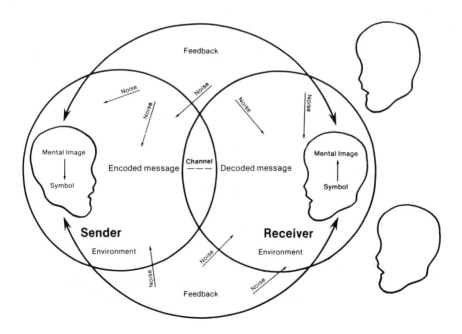

someone to see a movie with you Friday night. The beginning of this idea occurs with your mind "seeing" you and your friend at the theater. The next thing that happens is that you choose verbal and/or nonverbal symbols (i.e. words, gestures, etc.) to represent that mental image. The symbols you choose for the movie example might be to smile and say, "Sally, would you like to go see a movie Friday night?" The process of turning a mental image into a symbol is called **encoding**. Once you have completed the encoding process you have a message to send to another person. A **message** is the idea you want the other person to understand. Your encoded message must travel through some medium or **channel**. The channel may be *visual* as in eye to eye contact or watching the television, or it could be *audible* (heard). An example of the channel being audible would be two people in the same room talking, a telephone message or a radio broadcast. Once the encoded message travels through its channel, it finally arrives at its destination, the receiver. The **receiver** is the person you want to understand what you are saying. Just as the sender had to turn a mental image into a symbol, the receiver must now take that encoded message and turn those symbols back into a mental image. The process of turning a symbol into a mental image is called **decoding**. This process is the same whether you are speaking to one or several people.

Ineffective Communication

Far too often the message sent (encoded) is not the message received (decoded). For example, let's say you (the sender) wanted to describe a square to another person. You choose the symbols to use and send your message, but when the receiver decodes your message, his mental image is of a rectangle, not a square. Obviously the message sent was not the message received. There are three general reasons why this may occur.

1. The encoded message was unclear.
2. The sender and receiver did not share environments.
3. Noise interfered with the receiving of the message.

By looking at each of these causes of ineffective communication, we can see what occurs and lessen the likelihood of the message going astray. The encoded message was unclear. This means that the symbols chosen to represent the sender's mental image were not understandable to the receiver in the way intended. Perhaps he or she misinterpreted your meaning of a gesture or the definitions you meant for the words you chose. Another reason could be that in the process of encoding your message you left out some information you thought was obvious, but which your receiver was unaware of or didn't relate to.

The second cause of messages going astray is the sender and receiver did not share environments. **Environments** include everything there is about a person: physical characteristics, education, religion, home atmosphere, historical background, moods, etc. (represented on the diagram as circles around the sender and receiver). No two people share exactly the same environment because we are all individuals who are unique in many ways even though we overlap our environments in certain common areas. Sharing parts of our environments helps the sender and receiver understand each other. When our environments differ in the area we are trying to communicate about, very often that communication is ineffective. An example of differing environments and the misunderstanding that occurs might be as follows: The sender is awake and happy, while the receiver is tired and grouchy. The sender says, "Gee, you look nice today," meaning it as a genuine compliment. The receiver, because of her different environment, interprets it as a putdown and replies, "I suppose you mean I didn't look nice yesterday!" The message sent wasn't the message received.

The final cause of misunderstanding is noise interfering with the receiving of the message. **Noise** is any force that blocks communication due to lack of hearing (the physical act) or listening (understanding what is said). Noise is represented by arrows on the model. There are basically three general types of noise interference: external noise, internal noise and physical noise. *External noises* are sounds produced outside of your ears: factory machinery in operation, telephones ringing, children arguing, televisions blaring or other people talking which make it difficult to concentrate on what is said. External noises also include nonaudible interferences such as too hot a room, smoking or too uncomfortable a chair. External noise hinders our ability to hear or listen to what is said and may cause us to lose all or part of the message sent. *Internal noises* are the thoughts and feelings we are experiencing in our own bodies and minds. It is the noise between your ears. This refers to the times when you are preoccupied, daydreaming or worrying about an exam, and therefore don't listen to what is said. It is the time just after you had lost your father and someone who didn't know about your grief asks quite innocently, "How's your family?" The message may receive a hostile response because of your internal noise—grief. *Physical noise* refers to actual hearing problems or defects. A person who is hearing impaired because of an accident, from listening to loud music or simply from a bad cold will find it difficult to understand a verbal message. Any, all or a combination of the previously discussed causes may result in the message sent not being the message received. Being aware of how communication occurs and knowing where possible problems might occur will help you be a more effective speaker, whether you are speaking to a friend, your family or to your public speaking class.

A Communication Model

Purpose: The purpose of this exercise is three-fold. It will show that the speaker understands the process of communication, give experience in speaking and give the audience practice in using visual aids.

Procedure:
1. Design a communication model of your own that illustrates the process of communication.
2. Draw your model on a large poster.
3. Describe your model to your classmates, using your poster for clarification.

Listening: Its Definition and Importance

We have been talking about sending messages, but *communication is an exchange*. Communication requires you to receive messages, too. During this class, you will be both speaker and audience. Just as when you leave class you will need to understand, for example, the steps for making a new product at the plant where you work, to gauge when to sell or buy stocks for a profit or comprehend when your job is in jeopardy. All these instances imply the skill of listening, as well as talking. Listening is a skill that is very important and yet all too often taken for granted. People assume that if we can hear, we will listen. This is not always the case. **Hearing** is the reverberation of sound waves on the ear, i.e., the physical act. **Listening** is the willingness to understand oral communication. Just because we *hear* something doesn't mean we *listen* to it; in fact, we hear a large amount that we don't listen to.

There is more involved in listening than the appearance of paying attention. You may fool some people into thinking you are really

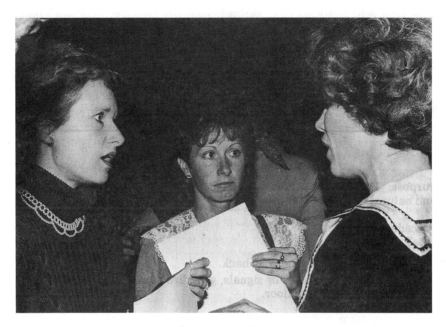

Listening is a large part of communicating.

listening to them when you're not, but you won't gain from the conversation or presentation what you may need. Some preparation for listening helps. The fact that people only speak at the rate of 150 words per minute and you can hear and assimilate 450 w.p.m. will leave lots of time for your mind to wander. The tendency will be for you not to pay attention, unless the message is geared to one of your favorite topics. We will usually listen to anything which involves us. We are our own favorite subject of conversation. Now, as clever as we all are, it seems obvious that we should be able to find something in the speaker's message that can relate to us. If we find that key, we will tend to listen with much more concentration.

Just think of all the time you are asked to spend listening in just one day. You listen to teachers, to coaches, to friends, and family. Because we tend to regard listening as a passive activity, most of us are terrible listeners. Although we receive careful instruction from our families about how to speak, we very seldom receive any instruction in listening. For that reason, in this class you will be asked to sharpen your skill in the art of listening. This art is part of the communication process, just as important as speaking.

As a speaker you will need to learn how to "listen" to nonverbal messages from your audience. A wrinkled forehead or a shake of the head can indicate that the last point you made was not clear or that your audience is not "buying it." They may yawn, or shift their weight in their seats, or lift their feet and play with the rungs of their chairs—all indications that you, the speaker, have lost them. They may nod in agreement and smile when you state something they believe to be true. Your audience is giving you **feedback** or message verification. Feedback is very important because you, as the speaker, need to be aware of your impact. The audience's responses will dictate the course of the speech, allowing you to rephrase your intention, add information for clarification or recast a conclusion.

All that is required to speak effectively is the skill to connect brain and mouth—a skill you already possess though you may not believe it. The task before you, then, is to develop a skill already partially conceived and courage which stems largely from your own intention. You may face rejection of your ideas. Any audience is free to accept or reject what is presented to them. In addition to subjecting yourself to rejection, you as a beginning speaker subject yourself to "stage fright," a malady which creates a kind of pressure that could turn you into a quaking mass of protoplasm.

Give a Eulogy

Purpose: The purpose of this speech is the same as the speech of introduction. It gives the student a beginning speech-making activity, provides information on the future audience, and can begin the process of interviewing.

Procedure:
1. Pair up with a classmate.
2. Talk with this person for 20 minutes or longer. Ask about their family, friends, favorite pastimes, life goals, etc. Then let them question you.
3. Prepare a two- to three-minute eulogy on your partner. A eulogy is a speech given upon the death of a person. It talks about their relationships, personal qualities and achievements in life. For the purposes of this exercise, you get to decide how and when your partner meets his demise. You can have them die today, perhaps from anxiety of having to give a speech, or a hundred years from now. You should also feel free to make it serious or amusing.
4. Present your speech.

Stage Fright: What It Is and What to Do About It

Consider this image: Giving a speech is like taking off your clothes in public. By definition, communication is very revealing. The exchange of thoughts, feelings and ideas implies the give-and-take aspect of communication. This give-and-take sometimes leads to rejection or at least the fear of rejection. This fear, **stage fright**, is one of the major concerns of most beginning and many experienced public speakers. Not everyone will buy every one of your ideas. If you have the freedom to express yourself, your listener should have the freedom to accept or reject what is being communicated.

What you fear as you take the podium for the first few times, however, is not a physical attack due to a rejection of your ideas. No college classroom is going to be turned into a battlefield with you dodging rotten tomatoes at the front of the room. No, what you fear—and the fear is entirely in your own head—is that you might appear a fool, one of the oldest horrors of childhood. You suffered the pangs of this fear in grade school when you were called upon to recite. Will I have the right answer? Does my teacher like me? Will my buddies tease me about it at recess? Regardless of whether you did your homework or not, you still were not certain, and any public exposure of your fragile ego made you sweat. (This is such a common problem that many communication scholars spend much of their time investigating *communication apprehension*.)

The same is true for you now, only now you have an ego which is older, bigger and probably more fragile. Your exposure to the world through that frantic period we call adolescence has taught you that you can be disappointed. You are sensitive. People out there possess the power to hurt you and you want no part of that suspected harm.

Let's look again around the room of your assembled speech class. All the other students will be required to get up and make speeches—the instructor requires it. Are they likely to be mean to you? Is it feasible that they would wish to hurt you? If they are getting up at that podium, too, won't they treat you as they would wish to be treated? Then, what is the problem?

The problem rests within your own mind. The audience is composed of sensitive people, who will be pulling for you all the way. For, in a certain sense, any failure on your part tends to be regarded by them as failure on theirs and they don't want to fail. So they don't want you to fail, either. But the psychological aspects—those thoughts floating around in your head—are only part of the picture of stage fright. There is also the physical aspect of the problem. What happens inside your body when stage fright strikes?

The physical reaction needs to be understood. What happens during an attack of stage fright is that adrenaline (a hormone produced by the body under stress resulting in superhuman strength) pumps through your body. This provides you with the kind of energy that allows a 125-pound woman to pick up an automobile if she sees her child pinned beneath it. This adrenaline surges through your body and must be released in some way. This is the same energy that gives you the added boost to run the 440 in 45 seconds. It is "the edge" coaches speak of in any athletic competition. What is the competition in speech? It is the struggle against those forces that would make you appear the fool. This

Fight stage fright by relaxing and doing some exercises.

energy will not just go away. It must be dissipated in some way. Often those ways our bodies choose to dissipate the adrenaline are most unattractive: we sweat, we shake, or we have dry mouth—all physical reactions to a source of energy which can provide nearly superhuman strength. Even professional actors suffer with this strange condition. They describe in great detail how they overcame the opening night jitters to go on to rave reviews.

You can deal with the physical symptoms of stage fright in a variety of simple ways. Dry mouth: pop a Lifesaver in your mouth to get the saliva glands working. This candy can be easily "stored" in your cheek and no one will be the wiser. Shallow breathing: consciously expand your breathing, slowly inhaling and exhaling. Feel your diaphragm expand. Knock-knee syndrome: rapidly tap your toe inside your shoe. Your body can expend a considerable amount of energy in this way, and the audience will be unaware of your movements. Once the energy is gone, your body will begin to relax. Panic: relax the entire vocal mechanism by yawning. This may sound impossible under the circumstances, but just let the jaw drop, inhale slowly, exhale slowly, just as you would with a yawn. Your neck and shoulder muscles will begin to relax. No one "uptight" can yawn.

Even with these practical suggestions for dealing with the physical symptoms of stage fright, another suggestion should be made. Attack the problem at its source: your mind. If the problem is basically a mental attitude (and it probably is), then what can you do to change your mind to help fix the problem?

You know people who always seem confident and poised. They are the ones who enter a room and seem immediately to size-up the situation and set about to join the group. Most of these people did not always behave in this manner. Often they began their interpersonal communications and public performance on as shaky and insecure foundations as those you are now experiencing. They may have felt awkward, or dumb or unprepared, too. What separates them from you is the attitude they consciously chose to adopt. Perhaps a line from Shakespeare is relevant here: "Assume a virtue if you have it not." If, after preparing your speech, and practicing it, and polishing the delivery, you still feel unsure, assume the cloak of one of those confident friends of yours. Act in a confident manner. After all, you've done all you can before the speech. The only thing left to do is to deliver it. Expect that the speech will go well. It's not quite as easy to believe that as to believe the reverse, but try it. Expectations go a long way to produce results in communication on any level. Set your mind for a positive outcome and much of the battle will already be won.

Before continuing with how speeches are prepared, researched and delivered, it is time to take a look at the three main styles of speech presentations.

Bring an Article

Purpose: The purpose of this exercise is to give the novice speaker a chance to speak about something he is familiar with. No research is required for this assignment which, therefore, allows the speaker extra time to prepare.

Procedure:

1. Decide on some article or item you have at home. It can be anything; something you are fond of or a common everyday item.
2. Prepare a three-minute speech about this item; simply describe it and/or relate its significance to you.
3. Present your speech in class.

Styles of Presentations

There are traditionally three ways that speeches can be presented: **impromptu speeches** require you to deliver your thoughts with little or no time for preparation; **manuscript speeches** are written word-for-word and read aloud; and **extemporaneous speeches** are prepared and practiced but allow room to adjust to the audience's reactions. Let's take an individual look at each style of presentation.

Impromptu Speeches

Most of you will want, at sometime or other, to express yourself in a meeting without a fully-prepared speech. Your Parent/Teacher Organization may be faced with the expenditure of some funds and you will wish to make known your desires for the use of that money. You will not have time to prepare. The group has been debating a motion and you feel you have some important input to the discussion. Simply gain the chairperson's attention and when you are called upon for your comment, rise and speak. The fear you will have is that some little gnome will crawl up your arm and remove a plug from your brain and release all your thoughts, leaving you with nothing to say. Nonsense! Your mind will continue to function. Your voice box and lungs will continue to work, and you will very possibly address a point that someone else, less brave than yourself, will wish he or she had. Believe in the free exchange of ideas which stands as the cornerstone of our democratic society: Men and women articulately and confidently expressing concern, warning or acceptance.

Obviously the impromptu speech has its place, in fact a great percentage of the communication we are involved in daily falls into this category. However, thinking on your feet is not as easy as it may seem. It takes practice to organize, support and deliver a speech that hasn't been given any real time to be developed. Because of this, it is inadvisable for beginning speakers to attempt this type of presentation except as an exercise for "getting their feet wet" in an in-class exercise. While it may appear to be easy and less time-consuming than preparing and practicing a more formal speech, it usually causes stage fright due to the feeling of "winging it" and not being prepared. This type of speech can also be rambling and illogical in its arguments since it is coming off the top of the head. Therefore it is not recommended as an appropriate presentation style for the majority of speeches given in a public speaking class.

Semi-Impromptu Speeches

Purpose: The purpose of this exercise is to give the beginning speaker a chance to speak without doing additional work.

Procedure:

1. Write down three topics you can speak about off the top of your head.
2. Have the instructor choose one of these topics.
3. Immediately give a three-minute speech on the chosen topic. Remain seated for this exercise.

Manuscript Speeches

These speeches are those which have been written word-for-word and are presented from a script. While there is a place for such speaking, we have tried in our classes to break the students from the habit of "writing a speech." Most of you will not be quoted in the newspaper or brought into court for expressing your beliefs, and therefore need not be this formal. Moreover, the manuscript speech tends to act as a barrier between speaker and audience. How many times have you been bored by a speaker who brought an entire sheaf of papers to the podium and droned on and on without once looking up to see if his message was being received or understood? Another problem that arises with manuscript-speaking is memorization. Often when a speech is written out word-for-word, the speaker then commits it to memory. This can lead to forgetting sections, embarrassment, not taking the audience's feedback into consideration and a "canned" vocal tone. To avoid this essay-on-its-legs approach we recommend the last type of speech—extemporaneous speeches.

Extemporaneous Speeches

These are speeches prepared in advance from an outline, practiced and delivered in private until a certain fluency has been developed. Then the notes and outline are put away and the unconscious mind of the speaker works on the material. On the day or evening scheduled for presentation, the speaker turns again to the outline and notes and gets the major points of the speech again in his or her conscious mind. As the speaker delivers the address, his/her eyes and mind are free to concentrate upon the audience— the real focus of the communication. When the number of quizzical looks on the audience's faces indicates that a point is obviously not being understood, the speaker is free to back up, change order, add details, whatever seems appropriate at the time to insure his audience's attention and illumination. Without a fully prepared, word-for-word script to read from, the speaker has a versatility and spontaneity which signals his or her audience that what they are enjoying is a fresh product of the speaker's mind working before them, and nothing is so exciting to an audience.

Before moving on to more specific techniques for presenting speeches we need to take a quick look at the three general types of speeches you may be asked to present.

The Informative Speech

This particular type of speech covers the majority of speeches you hear. We tend to believe our own information is most complete and that our friends and our colleagues are just dying to hear our explanation, feelings or philosophies. The **informative speech** is the one which has as its main purpose the transfer of knowledge from speaker to audience.

Since the goal of informative speaking is sharing data, it is important that the informative speaker must know precisely what he or she wants the audience to know at the conclusion of the speech.

Another important aspect of informative speaking has to do with audience analysis. Since you want not only to grab your audience's attention in the introduction, but maintain their attention through your conclusion, you must have a good idea of what their knowledge on your specific topic is likely to be. To keep your audience's interest you must aim at providing them with something new or explain something in a creative fashion that will hold their attention. A speech that is aimed above the general knowledge or below that knowledge will not be informative. At best, such a speech will serve as a review; at worst, you will totally lose the audience in boredom or confusion.

The Persuasive Speech

The type of speech often overlooked is the **persuasive speech**— that type of speech which attempts to produce some behavioral response or attitude alteration in an audience. Here lie the major rewards of this course. Once you have conquered your initial stage fright and mastered the principles of organization and research, you will be ready to attack an area of speech which can produce visible results. How do you get an audience to buy your product, vote for your motion or contribute money to your cause?

Persuasion need not be regarded as a dirty word or as the action of a con artist. Indeed few of us would ever donate blood if we hadn't been persuaded that there was a vital need for it, that it is not hazardous to our health, that it involves little time and/or that it is essentially painless. This type of speech is merely the process of getting your audience to think along the same lines as you. It is accomplished by providing your audience with enough clear, recent, significant reasons to accept your point of view.

Here is how persuasion is accomplished: You as the speaker provide your audience with an alternative to the way they are responding at present—a change from the status quo. You're asking them to use a new laundry soap, adopt a new school parking policy or support your motion in the Student Senate. In order to convince them of the merits of your proposal, you must provide three elements: (1) A need for a change, (2) a plan which meets that need, and (3) your audience's part in the change.

Persuasion, then, is the process of moving your audience from the point where all are thinking in different directions to the point where all minds are focused upon your arguments and are accepting your solution to the problem.

The Entertaining Speech

This is the type of speaking in which the speaker consciously works to place the audience at ease for the purpose of enjoying themselves. He or she makes the work of giving a speech look easy. The major purpose of the **entertaining speech** is to keep the audience's attention and interest for a short period of time, usually from 15 to 45 minutes. True, humor may be used, but a speaker need not be a comic to entertain an audience. Speeches dealing with the supernatural, genealogy or scuba diving, while apparently disseminating information, can be really entertaining.

This brief discussion of the three major types of speeches is to serve as a general overview. More detail is discussed in chapter seven.

Conclusion

You are now involved in the speech process. You have read that the rewards to you and others can be great. You know that you will be involved in this process as long as you live among people and that the fears of stage fright need not hamper you. Now that you are aware of presentation styles and types of speeches, let's get down to work.

Study Questions

1. Name three areas of your everyday life in which speech plays a significant part.
2. Describe and illustrate the communication process.
3. Name three reasons a message may be misinterpreted by the receiver, and tell what you could do to achieve effective communication.
4. What is the difference between listening and hearing?
5. What are some of the barriers to effective listening? What can you do to help you to listen?
6. How does stage fright affect you personally?
7. Name three physiological effects of stage fright and a remedy for each problem.

8. Why does your text recommend extemporaneous styles of preparation for most speeches?

Key Words

Channel

Communication

Decoding

Encoding

Entertaining speech

Environment

Extemporaneous speech

Feedback

Hearing

Impromptu speech

Informative speech

Listening

Manuscript speech

Message

Noise

Persuasive speech

Receiver

Sender

Stage fright

2 Preparation
How to Choose and Analyze a Topic

Chapter Two Outline

I. Here are some considerations as you choose a topic.
   A. Determine what you know.
   B. Assess what your audience may be expected to know.

II. Here are some hints on finding topics.
   A. Brainstorming is easy and fast.
   B. Don't overlook newspapers, television and magazines.
   C. We have included some general suggestions.

III. Thinking about your audience should be part of preparation.
   A. Perform an audience analysis.
   B. Interpret the results.

IV. Now you are ready to focus the topic.
   A. Focus for you.
      1. Find what you are interested in.
      2. Choose something you have knowledge about.
      3. Determine your general purpose.
         a. Your purpose is to inform.
         b. Your purpose is to persuade.
         c. Your purpose is to entertain.
   B. Focus for your audience.
      1. Determine what your audience is interested in.
      2. Determine what your audience knows.
      3. Determine what your audience's purpose for listening is.
   C. Focus for the occasion.
      1. Determine the length requirement of your speech.
      2. Consider the event at which you will speak.
   D. Focus for the environment.
      1. Take into account physical environment.
      2. Decide your equipment needs.

Chapter Two

Preparation:
How to Choose and Analyze a Topic

Introduction

Before you ever get up to the podium, before any of those awful symptoms of stage fright attack you, even before you dress for that occasion which you are sure will be your downfall—before any of the foregoing, you have to prepare. Any speaker who has successfully taken the podium has done considerable work before he ever got to that podium. Stop here for a moment and think of those people whose speeches have impressed you over the years: inspiring preachers, motivating teachers, stimulating public figures. What quality do these public speakers share? They all thought before they spoke. Here are some suggestions to get you started toward that goal of a successful speech.

Determine What You Know

In choosing a topic, the first thing you need to examine is *you*. What do you know that might be interesting to an audience? None of you live under a rock. Experiences happen to you every day: fascinating, funny, embarrassing, frightening events occur which would make excellent topics for short speeches. The major objective right now is to determine what you can already talk about without taking a month's worth of research to support. You may feel that nothing ever happens to you, but that's just not true. You could speak about a family member, an incident at work, a traffic problem you had getting to school, a new-found night spot. Any of these topics could be covered in a three- to five-minute speech. In addition, these topics involve you, a subject your audience will always find interesting, because we audience members are really "peeping Toms." We like knowing about someone else, not only the events themselves, but the significance that the speaker draws from the experience. You are not just rattling off a series of events for the audience. You are placing those events in a larger context, tying your experience to that of the audience. If I have an altercation with a sales clerk at the local hardware store, how can I turn that experience into a speech? I might talk about the rude clerks we have all encountered. I might speak about the pressures on the clerks when they are faced with an irate customer. I might discuss, in involved and humorous detail, how I had to return and apologize to the clerk when the plumbing part I insisted on buying didn't work as I thought it would. This speech subject happened to me; I do not have to look it up in the library.

Suppose you had an altercation with an instructor over a grade. We've all been in that situation, right? What can you tell your audience about this experience? What did you learn?

1. That talking to a professor is no big deal; he/she is just a person like me.
2. That verbally attacking a teacher about a grade made the instructor defensive—the same way I might become defensive when attacked.
3. That contact with the instructor outside of class may give me a greater understanding and appreciation of that teacher as an individual.

Any of the above three observations could be drawn and would make a worthwhile speech.

The point of this first speech is to get through it, not to deliver another Gettysburg Address. Probably none of these first speeches will wind up in print. Just determine what you want to share with your audience, something that will allow them to see and know you better. You are just breaking the ice.

Assess What Your Audience May Be Expected to Know

As you are choosing the topic, you must keep in mind that your audience is composed of people who have shared many of the experiences you will relate to them. This fact is a mixed blessing. It allows you to speak about things to which they can relate, but it requires that you not bore them by rehashing information they already possess. Think about what you can reasonably expect your audience to already know. Then find some detail which they may not be aware of. For example, we have all read and studied about the Declaration of Independence. Most people know that it was written in Philadelphia during the summer. What you may be able to add is that the summer of 1774 was one of the hottest on record. How would we behave if we had to sit in a stuffy, unair-conditioned hall debating the fate of our nation?

Most of us are aware of the basic rules of the game of baseball, but the fine points, regarding a close call in a World Series Game, may not be part of the audience's general knowledge. Simple common sense must apply here. Start with something familiar which your audience can grasp and then expand your coverage to include information which is *unique*. However, before any of these considerations come into play, we must first decide on a topic.

Finding the Topic: Brainstorming

One technique which often works to give you ideas is brainstorming. **Brainstorming** is an uncritical process used to stimulate thinking about topics. This is a process gained from Madison Avenue advertising campaigns. In attempting to devise a series of ads, the staff of a company will quickly list ideas as they occur to them in a group session. The key to brainstorming is to suspend judgment until a large number of ideas are collected. Here is one example of how it can work.

One large manufacturing company packed their goods for shipping by wrapping them in newspapers. This was an inexpensive method which appealed to the budget director. However, problems began to occur. The assembly line wrapping the packages began to slow down. Why? It was discovered that the people wrapping were reading the newspapers! A headline would catch their eye and instead of wrapping, they were reading. A committee was formed to solve the problem. The committee used the brainstorming method. They suspended all judgments and simply listed possible solutions. Their list included many ideas such as using foreign newspapers, using plain paper, using automation on the line, using illiterate workers, etc. After the brainstorming session, they went back and deleted ideas which would cost more money or lead to other problems. One of the suggestions was ''hire the visually handicapped.'' Although the idea was not meant seriously, that was exactly what the company did. Not only did they find an economic alternative, they received a government grant for hiring the handicapped! Brainstorming had provided a creative solution.

Brainstorming need not be done in a group, you can do it with

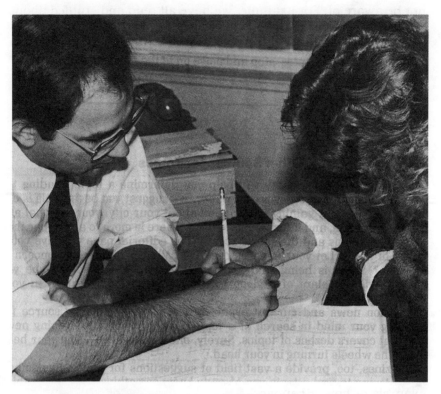

Brainstorm with a partner to find topics for speeches.

a friend or alone. Suppose you choose the general subject "school." What topics come to mind? The cafeteria, library, classes, teachers, grades, tests, sports? Perhaps you start with "my family." Brainstorm that topic: your uncle who drinks, your mother who advises, your aunt who gossips, your father who fixes things. After you have the list, you can cross off those which you feel would be inappropriate.

Brainstorm Topics

Purpose: The purpose of this exercise is to take the student through the process of choosing possible topics for speeches.

Procedure:

1. Divide the class into small groups of about five people.
2. Appoint a recordkeeper. If someone in the group takes shorthand, they're your person.

---

3. For 10 minutes, members of the group throw out possible topics while the recordkeeper writes them down. Keep in mind the following rules for brainstorming:
    a. Simply list ideas, don't judge them in any way.
    b. Hitch-hike off others' ideas. If one person says "Music," add ideas that stem off that like Rock, Big Band, Folk, Punk, etc.
    c. Remember your purpose is to compile as many topics as your group can list.
4. At the end of 10 minutes, stop and review your topics. This information will be used in later exercises on focusing.

Other Sources for Topics

One thing you do everyday will help you determine a topic: reading the newspaper. If you don't now read a paper, we suggest you begin. This is one of the best ways to gain information about your city, your national and state governments and international issues. There is more to any paper than the gossip columns and the sports scores. The editorial page will give you a number of ideas. Let your mind be creative. What is of current concern in your area? What is being said and written about that topic? Maybe you disagree with the slant of a given editorial and wish to refute it in your speech.

Television news and current events programs offer another source for triggering your mind in search of a topic. One thirty-minute evening news broadcast covers dozens of topics. Surely, one of those can inspire you and get the wheels turning in your head.

Magazines, too, provide a vast array of topics. Remember you are trying to find a topic you already know something about, something you'll not need to research to present a short three- to five-minute speech.

For the benefit of those who may like to have it, we have collected a list of topics (gained by our brainstorming) which might serve for this "icebreaker" speech. Notice many of these topics are oriented to your personal lives. We have done this to encourage you to share some of *you* with your new audience.

1. A favorite food, TV show or hobby.
2. The reason(s) you took this class.
3. An embarrassing incident.

4. Your family, pet or neighborhood.
5. A job or occupation you have performed or plan to perform.
6. A belief you hold about religion or politics.
7. Something you would improve about your school.

The One-Point Speech

Purpose: This exercise provides the speaker with practice in focusing on one central idea. It is a speech that states one proposition and illustrates it in a variety of ways.

Procedure:

1. Choose a proverb or familiar quotation as your speech topic.
2. Prepare any type of speech (informative, persuasive, or entertaining) on this topic.
3. Present a three- to five-minute speech.
4. Don't analyze your idea or break it into subpoints. By illustration, comparison or other means of clarification, impress the idea on your audience's minds. Try to avoid the actual statement of the quotation if possible, unless you can use it without appearing trite.

Possible Topics:

Plan ahead.
Don't cry over spilled milk.
The grass is always greener . . .
If at first you don't succeed . . .
A stitch in time saves nine.
An ounce of prevention is worth . . .
Early to bed . . .
Blood is thicker than water.
A penny saved is a penny earned.
Walk softly and carry a big stick.
We must hang together or surely . . .
No man is an island.
Behind every successful man, there is a woman.
If the shoe fits, wear it.
Man does not live by bread alone.
I came, I saw, I conquered.
The die is cast.
The early bird catches the worm.
I get by with a little help from my friends.
Beauty is only skin deep.

Nice guys finish last.
No news is good news.
Absence makes the heart grow fonder.
It's not if you win or lose, but how you play the game.
Blondes have more fun.
Haste makes waste.
It's not over 'til it's over.

With the topic in mind, at least tentatively, let's look at the audience who will hear you.

Audience Analysis

This term refers to a procedure you will perform so often that it will become second nature to you. **Audience analysis** is the process which involves gathering **demographics**—measurable

Your audience must be considered as you choose a topic for your speech.

information such as age, sex, occupation, etc.—about your listeners to insure their interest in your speech. It helps you to target shared experiences, knowledge, needs, ideas and goals in order to reach and keep your audience's attention. It is performed before you settle completely on a topic. Obviously you will give a different talk to a second-grade Sunday school class than a union meeting. Here is an exercise which will give you the profile of your class.

Exercise: Audience Analysis

Purpose: To understand the process of audience analysis so as to more accurately select a topic which will interest them.

Procedure:

1. Pair off and interview your partner about the following things:

   a. income
   b. political preference
   c. religion
   d. educational level
   e. gender
   f. favorite car
   g. favorite music
   h. favorite sport
   i. size of family

2. After you gather the information, pool the information on the front blackboard.

3. Analyze the results.

If you find that the majority of the class does not have any interest in politics (they vote "no preference"), then you know that you will have to work to get the audience to relate to a speech on a political issue.

NOTE: Audiences are both individual and collective. Many times your group will respond as a whole (like when they laugh at a good joke). But, there are also times when they will be quite individual, each person weighing your arguments and information by himself or herself and arriving at his or her own conclusions.

Now that you have performed an audience analysis on your class, remember that you will need to do this procedure for any audience you may be called to address, in or out of school. We'll have a little more to say about this process in the focusing section which follows.

Focusing

Now that you know a little bit about choosing a topic, it is time to begin the process known as focusing. *Focusing* means deciding on just one specific idea for your speech. Just as you focus the lens of a camera to photograph a clear image, you must focus your speech topic to have a clear concise speech. When you focus a camera, you first choose the proper lens for the type of photo you want; you adjust the lens until what you see is exactly what you want to appear in the picture. You decide whether you want a lot of background, producing a general view, or whether the subject of your composition will basically stand alone. You continue adjusting the lens until what appears in the viewfinder is precisely what you wish the developed photo to look like. Focusing a speech is accomplished in exactly the same way. You choose the approach and then proceed to adjust your topic until what you want in your finished speech appears in the topic. Another way of looking at the process of focusing is to think about it as narrowing your general speech topic.

Narrowing your topic from a broad subject to a specific idea is essential to presenting a well-prepared speech. Having one main idea in mind is necessary in preparing your speech. You could spend hours of unnecessary time researching a vague unfocused topic, accumulate massive amounts of information and be unable to use it, due to the type of speech or time imposed. You would waste your time and energy. Due to this lack of focusing, when it finally came time to present your speech, you would find it hard to follow and much longer than necessary. Working with one main idea in mind is necessary for research, organization and delivery. Perhaps a comparison will make it clearer to you why it is absolutely essential to focus and narrow your topic. Pretend you are going on a vacation and have a week before you must return. Let's say you live about a thousand miles from Orlando, Florida, and you would like to visit Disney World. However, you don't plan a day-to-day agenda. You start your trip on a southerly route and see whatever sites and entertainments you encounter along the way. Suddenly you realize you must be home in two days and you are still several hundred miles from Disney World. You must return home never having arrived at your original destination. An unfocused speech is very much like this type of vacation. While you may see many things along the way, you never quite get where you had planned.

To focus your topic you must take into account four factors (or considerations):

1. The *speaker* (you)
2. The *audience* (to whom you are speaking)
3. The *occasion* (the event at which you have been asked to speak)
4. The external *environment* (the facility and atmosphere in which you will be speaking)

These four categories overlap and will help you determine exactly what you want and need to include in your speech.

Assuming you have brainstormed for general topics, you must now start the process of focusing. The best place to start narrowing your topic is with yourself.

Focusing for the Speaker

Focusing with you as the speaker in mind, you must take into account three factors:

1. Choose a topic you are interested in.
2. Choose a topic you know something about.
3. Choose a topic that fits your general purpose.

Choosing a topic you are interested in is the most important decision a speaker makes. *The interest and enthusiasm a speaker brings to his or her topic is directly related to the interest the audience will give to the speech.* People talk about what they are interested in and know about. Billy Graham talks about religion, Siskel and Ebert talk about movies, Hilary Clinton talks about health reform and Shirley MacLaine talks about reincarnation. These people are well known and listened to because they show interest and enthusiasm about their topics. Their energy for their topics carries across in their delivery, making their speeches of interest to their audience. You can achieve success by following their example and picking a topic that interests you.

Once you've decided what you're interested in, you can begin to narrow the topic a little by deciding which of your many interests you wish to present. You may be interested in sky diving, but know little about the subject. Obviously, you can research the topic and learn something more, but usually for the beginning speaker, it is easier and safer to stick to something you already know. This doesn't mean that you won't need to do further research into the area, but it does give you a beginning framework for your speech.

So, now you have a list of interesting topics that you know about, and you're ready to proceed to step three of focusing for the speaker. You must now look at your list with the general purpose of your speech in mind. The general purpose will probably be one of these three (as shown in chapter 1):

1. To *inform* my audience (the transfer of information from speaker to audience)
2. To *persuade* my audience (getting the audience to think along the same lines as the speaker)

3. To *entertain* my audience (getting the audience to laugh or be amused with what the speaker says)

Let's say on your list thus far is the topic of voter registration and voting. This topic, depending on how you approach it, could fit into any of these categories. A speech on how to become a registered voter would be informative. A speech on why more people should vote in elections could be persuasive. An amusing story about an election could be entertaining. The most important aspect of focusing, at this point, is to know at which general purpose your speech is to be aimed.

Focusing for the Speaker

Purpose: The purpose of this exercise is to expand the speaker's imagination regarding topics he or she already knows.

Procedure:

1. Jot down three courses you especially enjoyed taking (in high school or college), or are currently taking. Take each course in turn and quickly note down these things about it:
   a. A fear you had before you took this course.
   b. One fact you learned in the course.
   c. One teaching technique you appreciated about the instructor.
2. Discuss with the class one of the courses you took.

Focusing for the Audience

The next step in focusing is to look at your audience. To do so you must take into account three questions:

1. What are the audience's interests?
2. What does the audience already know about the topic?
3. What is the purpose for your audience receiving this information?

Beginning public speakers often complain that they can't find a topic that their audience will find interesting. This view severely limits the scope of topics they choose for speeches. However, from looking at the data you have collected, you can see that the question is not so much, "What will my audience be interested in?" but rather "How can I make my topic interesting to my audience?" What follows is an example of focusing a topic for the audience's interests.

Tom was a student in a beginning public speaking course and had focused his topic for himself. He knew his interests were mainly sports, particularly football. His next step was to focus for his audience. He studied his audience and compiled several characteristics about them. He knew that the majority of his audience were women between 20 and 35 years of age. He also knew, from comments he had heard in the class, that many of them not only didn't understand football, but they were relieved to have somewhere else to go while their husbands watched Monday Night Football at home. How was Tom going to be able to interest them in a speech about football? He could have changed his topic, but he knew the golden rule of speech making was to speak on something which interested him. He decided to approach his topic in a creative way to interest his audience. Tom decided he would give his speech on the hand signals that the referee uses during a football game. But instead of simply relating the signals in the context of an actual football game, he made up a story and injected the signals into the appropriate places in his story. The story concerned a young couple on their first date at a drive-in movie. Tom told his story and each time the young man made some move that matched the type of hand signal a referee would use, he had the young lady use it. In one particular place in his story he had the young man make an amorous move toward the young woman. She then backed off and gave the hand signal for "fumbling." What Tom had done was take a topic he was interested in and approach it in such a way that it became interesting to his audience. In addition, it was both a humorous and informative presentation. So remember, just because your research indicates that your audience may not necessarily be interested in the topic you have chosen, you can make it interesting by approaching it in a novel, creative or useful way.

The next step in focusing for your audience is to try to answer the question, "What does my audience already know about my topic?" To answer this you will want to use the demographics you have collected as well as determine their general knowledge about your topic. It is important to determine what you can of the general knowledge of your audience. In this way you will know whether to speak on the basics (if you believe they know very little about your topic), or move on to more details (if you believe they already have a basic understanding of your topic). Topics such as abortion, gun control and capital punishment (common topics heard over and over in the media, as well as in the classroom) should either be discarded or approached in a creative way.

The last step in focusing for your audience is to determine the purpose your audience has in receiving your information. The way to do this is to find out (1) why they are gathered and (2) why you have been asked to speak to them. In the classroom situation the answers to these questions are obvious. The people are there to pass the course and have to give speeches to achieve a grade. However, most speaking engagements will not be in such an artificial environment. In public speaking situations your audience's reason for gathering is that they have something in common: they work at the same job and want to learn a useful new skill, or perhaps they enjoy needlepoint and want to learn how to make new designs. You must also be aware of any other reasons for which your audience has gathered that may not be specifically stated. These reasons are commonly referred to as a *hidden agenda*. For example, the stated reason for meeting might be to learn ceramics, but hidden agendas might be to meet new people, to have something to do on Wednesday night or any number of reasons not specifically related to ceramics. By trying to understand any hidden agendas and tapping into them you can further interest your audience in your topic.

The reasons you have been asked to speak to a group are these:

1. You can fulfill their need to learn something that you are qualified to speak on (an informative speech).
2. You can share your views on certain issues (a speech to persuade).
3. You can amuse them (an entertaining speech).

Knowing the purpose for the audience's gathering and why you have been asked to speak to them will help determine not only your topic but the approach as well.

Just a few words of caution seem appropriate before moving on to focusing for the occasion. When you are preparing your speech, keep in mind that you must be careful not to offend your audience and make them hostile to receiving your information: (1) Don't insult your audience's intelligence by speaking down to them; (2) Don't speak over their heads, making them feel dumb or like children; (3) Be very careful not to offend or exclude any member of your audience on the basis of his/her sex, religion or racial heritage. A speaker who doesn't follow this advice may find himself or herself the target of the audience's anger, which makes speaking to them difficult, if not impossible.

Focusing for the Audience

Purpose: This exercise is designed to emphasize the point of view of the audience as the speaker determines his or her topic.

Procedure: Choose one of the following topics. (Remember to pick one about which you know something. You must first focus for the speaker.)

1. A popular sport: baseball, football, soccer.
2. A popular pastime: watching TV, listening to music, dancing.
3. Preparing for an interview for a new job.

After you have picked a topic, quickly jot down three things which you believe everyone will know about the topic. Then, follow that list by devising three things which not everyone knows about the topic. Check your list against the whole class to see if you were accurate in your assessment of what your audience can be expected to know.

Focusing for the Occasion

To focus your topic for the occasion you need to ask yourself two questions:

1. How long is my speech supposed to be?
2. For what event am I speaking?

How long is your speech supposed to be? This is the time limit you must work with. Timing your speech is very important. If you are asked to speak for 10 minutes, your audience will expect to hear you speak for that length of time, not 5 minutes, not 20 minutes. The time limit that you have been given is one of the most limiting requirements in focusing your topic. Start with how long your speech is to be, and then decide what you can adequately cover in that length of time. Your topic should be broad enough to fill that time, yet specific enough to avoid leaving out necessary parts of your speech. For example, you are to give a five-minute speech and have decided that the general topic of your speech is the Civil War. You've focused your topic for yourself and your audience and now must consider your time limit. Obviously, you can't cover the entire Civil War in five minutes. You must narrow the topic so that it can adequately be covered in five minutes. In the time limit given, you could probably discuss one particular battle, or a certain general.

In doing this you have focused on a specific topic.

Once you have narrowed your topic to the time limit, you must again look at the event or purpose for your speech. The event could be an annual awards banquet, a Christmas dinner or a gathering of Parents Without Partners. Knowing why you and your audience are there will tell you the general direction your speech should take. Remember, your purpose is to get and keep your audience's attention.

Focusing for the Occasion

Purpose: The purpose of this exercise is to concentrate attention on the event at which you are to speak.

Procedure:

1. Choose three of the following occasions and jot down a topic which you would feel comfortable speaking about for such a function.

    a. The end-of-the-year awards banquet.

    b. The final meeting of this speech class.

    c. A major religious holiday speaking to a group at your church or synagogue.

    d. A celebration of a national holiday, i.e., Fourth of July, Memorial Day, Thanksgiving.

2. Share your selection of topics with the class for reactions.

Focusing for the Environment

The last step in focusing your topic is to consider the physical environment (surroundings) in which you will be speaking. Will you be speaking in a large auditorium, a small intimate living room or at a conference table? What facilities will be available to you? Is there a microphone, space for flip charts, an opaque projector or maybe even other props such as a microwave oven to demonstrate a cooking technique? Knowing where you will speak, what will be available to help you explain your topic and the general atmosphere of the gathering will further determine what you will cover in your speech.

Focusing for the Environment

Purpose: The purpose of this exercise is to determine the physical needs the speaker must consider when speaking in various places.

Procedure: If possible move the class to various locations on campus. If not, try to imagine yourself in these different locations: a larger lecture hall, a small room, the gym, the lobby of your theater, outside under the trees. Vary the relationship of the audience to the speaker. Place the speaker in the middle of the group. Move the speaker twenty-five or fifty feet away from the group. Introduce distractions to the audience which the speaker will have to overcome, i.e., play a radio in the background. If possible try to allow the speakers to work with a microphone to hear their voices amplified. Discuss the results of these various excursions.

Perhaps the process of focusing your topic seems long and involved to you, but remember this: The better prepared you are for giving your speech, the easier and smoother the presentation will go.

Preparing for your speeches is essential.

Let's summarize the focusing process.

1. Choose a topic which you are interested in, which you know something about and which fits your general purpose (to persuade, entertain or inform).
2. Focus your topic for your audience by taking into account their characteristics as a group, their general knowledge and their purpose for receiving your information.
3. Narrow your topic by knowing what you can cover in the time limit and the reason for presenting your speech.
4. Know what the physical environment will be where you will be speaking. Take into account the space, facilities and atmosphere of the speaking situation.

Conclusion

As you can see by now, the process of getting up and giving a speech is a bit more complicated than just throwing some thoughts on some note-cards and jumping up to a podium. In order to make a success of public speaking the speaker must consider other people and numerous circumstances. By regarding topic choice, focusing and thoughtfully considering your audience, we promise you your rewards will be attention, understanding and a wonderful bond growing between you and those who are sharing in this unique communication process.

Study Questions

1. List three possible speech topics of which you have knowledge.
2. Why must a speaker consider the audience's general knowledge when choosing content for his/her speech?
3. What is the importance of audience analysis in determining the approach to your topic?
4. Name the four considerations in focusing a topic.
5. Define brainstorming. Why is it useful?
6. Choose a topic and indicate exactly what you would do to focus it.

Key Words

Audience analysis	Focusing
Brainstorming	Hidden agenda
Demographics	

3

Specific Purpose, Outlining, Introductions and Conclusions

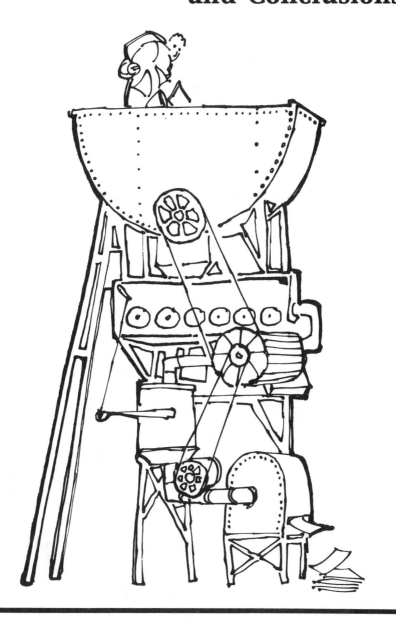

Chapter Three Outline

I. A specific purpose is a simple sentence that states the response the speaker wishes the audience to have at the end of his speech.

    A. It must be written as a simple statement, a complete sentence.

    B. It must be worded clearly and concisely.

    C. It must be worded so that it states what the audience's response will be.

II. A well-prepared speech is organized through the use of a well-developed outline.

    A. There are two categories of outlines.

        1. Working outlines are used by the speaker and need not follow any specific style.

        2. Formal outlines are presented to the instructor and must follow certain rules.

            a. Major divisions are noted by Roman numerals.

            b. Subpoints are noted by capital letters.

            c. Sub-subpoints are noted by Arabic numbers.

            d. Any further divisions are noted by small letters.

            e. Supporting materials are noted as the type of support they are.

    B. There are many ways of dividing and ordering main points.

        1. They may be listed in chronological order.

        2. They may be listed in spatial order.

        3. They may be listed in process order.

        4. They may be listed in priority order.

        5. They may be listed in any other order that helps the speech move logically from point to point.

    C. Three items are added to the outline after completion.

        1. The introduction precedes the formal outline.

        2. The conclusion follows the formal outline.

        3. The source materials are listed last on the outline.

III. Creating an effective introduction and conclusion is essential to presenting an effective speech.

    A. An introduction must meet three requirements:

        1. It should gain the audience's attention.

        2. It should tell the audience what the subject matter will be.

        3. It should tie the speaker to the audience.

    B. There are many ways of beginning a speech.

        1. You may begin by giving an example or telling a story.

   2. You may begin by asking the audience a question.
   3. You may begin by presenting a quotation.
   4. You may begin by referring to a historical event or date.
   5. You may begin by telling a joke.
   6. You may begin by stating an unusual fact.
   7. You may begin by using a gimmick.
   8. You may begin by referring to the purpose of the gathering.
C. An effective conclusion must do three things.
   1. It re-emphasizes the main point of your speech.
   2. It climaxes your speech by tying everything together.
   3. It leaves your audience remembering what you said.
D. There are many ways of concluding a speech.
   1. You may end in any of the ways listed for beginning a speech.
   2. You may end by summarizing what has been said.
   3. You may end by giving an invitation to the audience to look toward the future.
   4. You may end by calling the audience to action.

Chapter Three

Specific Purpose, Outlining, Introductions and Conclusions

Introduction

You now have a good idea of how to choose a topic for a speech and how to focus that topic into a workable idea. The next step in the process that will eventually lead you to the presentation is a manner of organizing and refining that topic. This will allow you to define exactly what you want your audience to know or do at the conclusion of your speech and how you will arrive at that destination.

Preparing and Writing the Specific Purpose of the Speech

After focusing your speech topic, the next step in the preparation is to write a specific purpose for your speech. A **specific purpose** is a simple sentence that states the response the speaker wishes the audience to have at the end of the speech. It states the final goal of the speaker, the one response the speaker wishes from the audience. A specific purpose is very similar to a thesis sentence prepared for an English composition. In the length of one simple sentence you will state the intent and desired goal of your entire speech.

A specific purpose is arrived at in much the same manner as the topic was focused. A specific purpose not only reflects the speaker's interests, knowledge and goals, but also takes into account the audience's interests, the occasion and the environment. Once you have your topic focused, you then compose a specific purpose.

A specific purpose should follow these guidelines:

1. It must be written as a simple statement, a complete sentence.
2. It must be worded clearly and concisely.
3. It must be worded so that it states what the audience's response will be.

Looking at each of these guidelines individually, we can learn how to write a clear and effective specific purpose. The first guideline is *A specific purpose must be written as a simple statement*. A complete sentence means that you must include one, and only one, subject in your statement. "The audience will be able to make a banana split" is a simple sentence. "The audience will be able to make a banana split and I will show them the best way to eat it" is a compound sentence and, therefore, doesn't meet the requirements of a specific purpose. This doesn't mean that you may not have to cover more than one item or section in your speech (depending, of course, on the time limit you have), but it does require you to be specific about the ultimate goal of your speech. That goal should be worded as one item. You may have to talk about several ideas to reach that goal, but ultimately your goal is one, and only one, accomplishment.

Inherent in this first requirement, that a specific purpose is a complete sentence, is that it has a subject (who or what is doing the action of the sentence) and a verb (the action taking place). "To inform about squirrel hunting," is a sentence fragment, not a complete sentence and therefore doesn't fit the requirement. Because of the last requirement for specific purposes, being worded to the audience's response, the subject of all specific purposes will be the audience. It will be the audience that is doing, knowing, being informed, etc. in the sentence. Example: "The audience will know how to hang wallpaper." The verb is "will know how to hang." Who or what will know? The audience will know. By locating the verb in the statement and asking "Who or what is doing the action of the verb?" you will discover what the subject is and be assured that you have a complete sentence. Remember that for specific purposes, the answer to that question will be the audience.

The second guideline, *A specific purpose must be worded clearly and concisely*, means that your specific purpose should be easily understood. You should make your statement as short as possible and use words or phrases that say *exactly* what you want the audience to know. "The audience will know about the Federal Reserve System," is not worded clearly and concisely. It is written in the proper form, but it does not show that the speaker knows precisely what he wants from his audience. What specifically about the Federal Reserve System does he want his audience to know? Should they know how or why it was formed, its purpose, what effect it has on our economy or why it should be changed or abolished? A clearer purpose would relate to one of these latter areas, not the vague concept of "knowing about the Federal Reserve System." Therefore, a specific purpose for an informative speech on this topic might be "The audience will know why the Federal Reserve System was founded." A specific purpose for a persuasive speech might be "The audience will be convinced that the Federal Reserve System should be abolished."

Another weakness to avoid is the use of too many adjectives in your specific purpose. "The audience will know the recipe for chocolate chip cookies," fits the requirements for a specific topic. Adding "delicious, home-baked with love" would be too flowery and inappropriate, distracting from the clarity of the goal.

The third guideline, *A specific purpose must be worded so it states what the audience's response will be*, means that your specific purpose should refer to what you want your audience to know or do at the completion of your speech. "I want to tell my audience to donate blood to the Red Cross" does not include a response from the audience. It states what the speaker will do, but it does not state that the audience will donate. "The audience will donate blood during the next bloodmobile drive," states exactly what the audience will do. This requirement may seem unimportant or nit-picky, but actually there is an important reason for doing it this way. Stating that you are going to talk about something only requires you to speak. It does not actually require you to inform, persuade or entertain.

When you state you are going to inform, tell, motivate, persuade or convince your audience, you are referring to what you as the speaker will be doing in your speech. Obviously, this is your purpose in giving any speech. However, the third requirement of a specific purpose is to get you to approach your speaking assignment in such a way that you focus on how you will persuade, entertain or inform your specific audience. Therefore, it is very important that you state that specific purpose of what you want from your audience at the conclusion of your speech. Writing the specific purpose in this manner forces you to consider the audience with a knowledge of how they individually and collectively can and will be motivated to achieve the goal you have established.

Simply speaking, little or no consideration of your audience's response leads to a vague and unfocused speech. Knowing precisely how you want your audience to respond helps create a directed and effective speech. After all, your purpose in giving your speech must be to reach your audience and interest them in what you are saying; otherwise, you might as well be speaking to an empty room.

Examples of Properly Worded Specific Purposes

Remember that the subject of a specific purpose will be your audience. They are the ones who will ultimately be responsible for the action, knowledge, etc., you wish to achieve at the conclusion of your speech. Examples:

1. The audience will know how to change a flat tire.
2. The audience will know how to register to vote.
3. At the conclusion of my speech the audience will sign a petition against raising gasoline taxes.
4. The audience will agree that the people of Poland should be allowed to strike for better working conditions.
5. The audience will be amused with my story about canoeing.

Specific Purpose Exercise I

Purpose: The speaker will learn how to write a specific purpose.

Procedure:

1. Choose one of the topics your group had at the completion of the Focusing exercises.
2. Write a specific purpose for this topic. Make sure it follows the three rules for a specific purpose.
   a. It must be written as a simple sentence.
   b. It must be worded clearly and concisely.
   c. It must be worded so that it states what the audience's response will be.
3. Submit your written specific purpose for your instructor's comments.

There are a few more factors that need to be understood about the process of preparing specific purposes. Specific purposes follow the same guidelines whether they are speeches to inform, persuade or entertain; however, because of the intent of the speaker and the nature of the goal, they may be worded differently. When you are giving a speech in which the general purpose is to inform, what you are doing is transmitting data. You are not required to get your audience to change a belief or perform any action other than understand what is being said. "The audience will know . . ." "The audience will understand . . ." "The audience will have a clear knowledge of . . ." In a speech to persuade, you are not merely passing along information, but are trying to get your audience to take some kind of action. The specific purpose must reflect this fact: "The audience will believe . . ." "The audience will sign . . ." "The audience will donate . . ." Remember that in a persuasive speech you may have to inform your audience, but your ultimate goal is to achieve some particular action or movement on their part. Make sure your specific purpose states that result.

It is important to note that the specific purpose will probably not be stated to the audience directly in your speech. It is a tool for you to use to make sure you achieve your goal. We suggest that the specific purpose be included in the formal outline, usually placed directly preceding the Introduction. Writing down the specific purpose seems to cement it in the speaker's mind and helps him or her reach such a conclusion.

The following is a checklist of questions that you can use to make sure the specific purpose you have written fulfills all the criteria.

1. Is it a complete sentence, i.e., does it have a subject and a verb?
2. Is the subject of the sentence the audience, i.e., are they the ones doing the action of the verb?
3. Does it satisfy the focusing process, i.e., is it still the clear idea you had after considering the speaker, audience, environment and occasion?
4. Can this goal be achieved in the time limit given?
5. Does it state exactly what you want the audience to know or do?

The importance of preparing a properly worded specific purpose should not be ignored. A well-worded, carefully directed specific purpose often marks the difference between a speech which is understood, and a wandering monologue that interests no one but the speaker.

Specific Purposes Exercise II

Purpose: The purpose of this exercise is to give the student practice in preparing different types of specific purposes.

Procedure: Below you will find examples of specific purposes for focused speeches. After each specific purpose please fill in "b" with another specific purpose for that speech.

Examples:

> Type of Speech: three- to five-minute informative speech
> General Topic: Halloween

a. The audience will know how to carve a jack-o-lantern.

b. (You fill this in) The audience will be able to make popcorn balls as treats for Halloween visitors.

Exercises:

1. Type of Speech: three- to five-minute informative speech
   General Topic: Snow
   a. The audience will know how to make a snowball.
   b.

2. Type of Speech: three- to five-minute informative speech
   General Topic: Clothes
   a. The audience will be able to construct a wrap-around skirt.
   b.

3. Type of Speech: three- to five-minute informative speech
   General Topic: Zoos
   a. The audience will be aware of how the St. Louis Zoo is funded.
   b.

4. Type of Speech: five- to seven-minute persuasive speech
   General Topic: Valentine's Day
   a. The audience will send Valentine's Day cards to their loved ones.
   b.

5. Type of Speech: five- to seven-minute persuasive speech
   General Topic: Cars
   a. The audience will prefer purchasing an American-made car rather than a foreign-built car.
   b.

6. Type of Speech: five- to seven-minute persuasive speech
   General Topic: Cleaning
   a. The audience will use Comet cleaner instead of Ajax cleaner.
   b.

7. Type of Speech: three- to five-minute entertaining speech
   General Topic: Picnics
   a. The audience will enjoy my story about picnicking in the snow.
   b.

8. Type of Speech: three- to five-minute entertaining speech
   General Topic: Finger painting
   a. The audience will have fun learning how to make finger paints.
   b.

9. Type of Speech: three- to five-minute entertaining speech
   General Topic: Vacations
   a. The audience will be amused by the mishaps that occurred on my trip to Washington, D.C.
   b.

You may wish to get some help in forming your outline.

Outlining the Speech

You've chosen a topic that you're interested in, focused that topic, and written a specific purpose for your speech. Now you're ready to actually begin preparing the main parts of your speech.

The key to developing a well-prepared speech is *organization*. Organizing your speech means arranging your material in a manner that is orderly and easy to follow. Outlining is the process we use to achieve this goal.

There are five main benefits to preparing a well-developed outline:

1. You will remember your speech better.
2. You will be more relaxed knowing you are prepared for your speaking assignment.
3. Your audience will be better able to follow what you say because it will move logically from idea to idea.
4. Your audience will be interested in what you say.
5. Your audience will remember what you said.

There are two categories of outlines: (1) working outlines and (2) formal outlines. **Working outlines** are what the title implies; they are outlines used when "working" on your speech. These are used to help you organize your ideas. They assist you in putting your information in order and deciding what to include to support each main point of your speech. These outlines can be written in any style you choose, any way that is easy for you. These outlines will probably be seen only by you, and therefore, need not follow any specific style.

A **formal outline** is the one you will present to your instructor when you give your speech. This outline can be written in several styles, but it must conform to certain rules. We will look at two styles of outlining that seem to work best for the beginning public speaker. These are "topic" and "full-sentence" outlines. Both of these styles follow this same basic format. Here is the formal style:

I.
    A.
        1.
        2.
            a.
            b.
    B.
II.

All major divisions (main points) of your speech are noted by Roman numerals (I, II, III); subpoints by capital letters (A, B, C); sub-subpoints by Arabic numbers (1, 2, 3); and any further division by lowercase letters (a, b, c). If you find it necessary to divide any points further, it probably means that your topic is too broad and needs to be more clearly focused.

When deciding on the major divisions of your speech, you must take into account what the primary (most important) sections of your speech are. They should be equal in importance and fill about the same amount of time in your presentation.

Example: You are giving a speech about domestic cats. Your main points might look like this:

   I. Siamese
  II. Persian
 III. Calico
 IV. Alley

Subpoints represent a division of main points; they further explain those points. These should also be of equal importance and relate specifically to the heading they fall under. In the same way, sub-subpoints fill the requirements for the category (subpoints) that they are dividing. At this point, it is important for you to understand that because the process of outlining involves breaking down "wholes" into smaller sections, each time you make a division, you must break it down into at least two parts. Simply stated, this means every time you have an A, you must have at least a B; for every 1 there must be a 2.

Occasionally, you may find that some of your supporting material does not easily fall into two or more sections, but that it is necessary to the development of your topic. When this occurs, instead of denoting 1's and 2's or a's and b's, you simply identify them under the section they relate to. This is done by labeling the type of support they are—such as example, story, quotation, definition or visual aid—and following it with a colon.

Let's take a look at an example of the previously discussed principles of outlining:

Your topic is "How to Change a Flat Tire."

Your specific purpose is, "The audience will know how to change a flat tire."

   I. Equipment
      A. Tire Tool
         Visual Aid: show tool
      B. Jack
         1. Type A (bumper)
         2. Type B (scissors)
      C. Spare Tire

  II. Procedure
      A. Securing the Vehicle
         1. Pull car off road
         2. Make car immovable
            a. Put transmission in park
            b. Block wheels
               Example: chocks or bricks
      B. Removing the Flat Tire
         1. Remove hubcap
         2. Loosen lug nuts
         3. Jack up car
         4. Remove tire
      C. Replacing the Tire
         1. Put wheel on rim
         2. Replace lug nuts
         3. Release jack
         4. Tighten lug nuts
         5. Replace hubcap
      D. Finishing the Job
         1. Put equipment away
         2. Remove wheel blocks

    3. Go to the nearest service station
      a. Have lug nuts tightened
      b. Check air pressure in spare
      c. Have flat fixed

Notice the form of the outline; where to indent, what to capitalize and where to put periods. This outline is written as a topic outline; that is, it uses words and phrases for each division. The second style of outlining uses the same form, but instead of words or phrases it uses complete sentences. This is appropriately called a sentence outline (for an example of this style of outlining, refer to the outlines at the beginning of each chapter in this text). Either style is usually acceptable in a formal outline. Most people find it easiest to use the topic outline, but many beginning speakers like the added security of a full-sentence outline (particularly if their outline stands as their notes to speak from). Whichever style you choose, be consistent. Use only topics or sentences throughout the outline; don't interchange. (Note: If you are typing or using a computer for outlines, the Roman Numerals are made with capital "i" (I) and "v" (V).

    There are many ways of dividing and ordering your main points. The most important thing to remember is to prepare your outline so that your speech will move from point to point in a logical and easily-understood progression. In learning how to decide the order, let's look at four ways of organizing:

    1. Chronological Organization (time)
    2. Spatial Relationships (space)
    3. Process Organization (steps)
    4. Priority Organization (Importance)

    Chronological organization means that your material is placed in a time frame. What occurred first, second, third? You move from the beginning through the most recent occurrence. If you were speaking on the development of our money system, your chronological divisions might look something like this:

    I. Ancient Barter System
   II. Early Roman Coinage
  III. English Money
  IV. Colonial Money
   V. Modern Money

All divisions made in respect to time are chronological, whether they refer to years, months or minutes.

    Spatial organization implies that divisions are made according to geographical space or area. If you were speaking about taking a trip from New York to California your spatial divisions might be like this:

  I. Leave New York
 II. Drive to Pennsylvania
III. Continue to Missouri
 IV. Go to Colorado
  V. Arrive in California

Remember any division that moves from place to place or requires an arrangement involving space is spatial.

Process organization is used when you wish to follow a certain series of actions step-by-step. An outline on how to bake a cake could be handled in this way:

  I. Read the recipe
 II. Collect the ingredients
III. Collect the utensils
 IV. Mix the ingredients
  V. Bake the cake
 VI. Serve

Any division that refers to step-by-step actions is a process division.

Priority organization separates items by importance; least to most or the reverse. You must decide early in your preparation what you want to have the most importance. An outline for priority of personal hygiene could look like this:

  I. Cosmetics
 II. Body cleanliness
III. Protection from sexually transmitted diseases

There are several other ways to divide your topic. Just make sure that the divisions you make help the flow of your speech. The speech must move logically and smoothly from point to point.

The question often arises as to exactly how much information should be included in a formal outline. The easiest answer to that is, if you're going to speak on it, include it. A good outline is one that exhausts the data to be covered. An outline of a speech is much like a map. If you were drawing a map, you would want it to be clear enough for someone to use while traveling. Your outline is used in the same way, it directs the flow of your speech and includes all data used to express your specific purpose. Your outline is now almost complete. It simply requires the addition of three other ingredients: the introduction, the conclusion and your sources. These we'll cover now.

Put It In a Logical Order Exercise

Purpose: The purpose of this exercise is to give the student an opportunity to gain experience in organizing data.

Procedure:

1. Organize the following statements in a logical order.
2. Statements:
   a. Channeling is part of the New Age.
   b. The New Age is the belief that each individual creates his/her reality through beliefs and thought processes.
   c. A belief in a higher power is part of the New Age philosophy.
   d. There really is nothing "new" about the New Age.
   e. Shirley MacLaine is a strong proponent of the New Age philosophy.
   f. Here are some of the beliefs of the New Age.

All speeches have three main parts: the introduction, the body and the conclusion.

Thus far we have outlined the body of your speech. Now, having what material you will cover, and in what order you will present it, it is time to consider how you will begin and end your speech. It may seem strange to write your introduction after you have completed the main part of your speech, but there is an important reason for doing so. You must know what you are going to say before you can decide how you will initially inform your audience about it. Introductions and conclusions will be covered in detail in a later section of this text. Right now we are concerned with their proper placement in the outline.

There are several ways of including your introduction and conclusion in your outline. We will suggest two ways that have been successful for our students. The first is, immediately preceding the outline of the body of the speech, write "Introduction" and follow this word with a brief description of what you will say. For example, "Introduction: Story about my meeting Mickey Rooney," (or) "Introduction: Quotation: 'Ask not what your country can do for you, but what you can do for your country.' (John F. Kennedy Inaugural Address, 1960)." The conclusion is handled in the same manner, only it follows your outline. "Conclusion: Mickey Rooney may be short in stature, but he's tall in my book!" (or) "Conclusion: Quotation: 'Some men see things as they are, and ask "why?" I dare to dream of things that never were, and ask "why not?"' (Robert Kennedy)."

The second form is specifically developed for writing speeches. Since all speeches have an introduction, body, and conclusion it is logical that the outline's main points be labeled and arranged in that order.

   I. Introduction
  II. Body
 III. Conclusion

You then break down each part of the speech under the main points (Roman numerals). This style of outlining has an advantage of focusing in on the importance and purpose of each section of the speech. While the time spent on the delivery of the body of the speech will be the largest percentage and obviously longer than the introduction and conclusion, this style emphasizes the equal importance of the three sections in achieving the goal of the speech.

The last thing you must include on your outline is your list of sources. This should be done in standard bibliography style (see Chapter 4 on how to write a bibliography) and include all references used. Please note that "sources" is intentionally plural. How many sources you need for a particular speech will vary, but it should be obvious to you that the days of copying information from one source and presenting it as your "oral report" are long gone. The only possible exception to this statement is when you are relating a personal experience. Even though some speeches draw on your own knowledge, very often that knowledge originated with some other source. After all, someone showed you how to change the oil in your car, you learned how to type from a manual or your "original" recipe started with a basic one. Giving credit to the sources of your information is necessary to support your information.

Here is a summary of what to do to write an outline:

1. Decide on your major divisions.
2. Divide the major items, where necessary, into further categories.
3. Use the proper form and be consistent in style.
4. Make sure your order is logical.
5. Include all pertinent information you will be speaking on.
6. Fill in your introduction, conclusion and sources.

With a well-organized outline, your speech is now ready to become an oral presentation.

Outlining Exercise

Purpose: The purpose of this exercise is for the student to learn how to write a formal outline.

Procedure:
1. Outline a manuscript speech recommended by your instructor. You may use a full sentence outline or a topical outline.
2. Submit your outline to the instructor for comments and corrections.

Beginning and Ending Your Speech:
Introductions and Conclusions

Research shows us that your audience will listen best to the beginning and the end of your speech. Therefore, creating an effective introduction and conclusion is essential to presenting an effective speech.

The **introduction** of your speech must be planned and prepared to ensure that you start out in a positive, productive manner, and should fill approximately 15 percent (or less) of your time limit. An effective introduction must fulfill the following three criteria:

1. It gains the audience's attention.
2. It tells the audience what the subject matter will be.
3. It ties the speaker to the audience, giving them a reason to listen.

Gaining the audience's attention is vitally important to accomplishing any speaking goal you may have in mind. If you don't grab their attention and get them to listen to you in the beginning, chances are you won't be able to catch them at all. The attention-getter that you use must, however, also fulfill the other two criteria.

In a speech class several years ago, a student used an attention-getter that really got his audience's attention, but failed miserably in the other two categories. Bill began his speech by dropping a lit match into a wastebasket filled with paper. The materials took flame and set the sprinkler system off in the classroom. Obviously, it was necessary to evacuate. Even though he won the attention of his audience, they didn't know that his topic was on stage lighting. So, your introduction must not only get your audience to pay attention to you, but also must present your topic to them. The third requirement for an effective introduction is to tie you, the speaker, to them. This means showing your audience why you and they are sharing a common experience or interest. What you want to accomplish by doing this is to win them over to your side and show them why it is important for them to listen to you. You want them to be concerned, excited, happy or angry (*with* you, not *at* you). To do this you must simply alert your audience to what it is you have in common. For example, a speech on how to prepare a certain meal would tie you together because everyone eats.

There are many ways to start your speech. The more original and creative you are the better. All too often beginning speakers have a tendency to begin with "Today I'd like to tell you about . . ." While there is nothing technically wrong with this style of introduction, it does lack in the attention-getting department, and it's dull! What follows is a list of possible ways to begin your speech that have proven to be effective when used the right way.

1. Give an example, or tell a story.
    a. "It was snowing heavily, and I was on my way home from a late night appointment. Suddenly, my car skidded into a snowbank, and I couldn't get unstuck. I was on a deserted stretch of highway and it was only four degrees outside."
    b. Teaching someone how to do something is often the best way to learn. For example: "You've been studying algebra and think you understand it fairly well. Your younger brother is taking a beginning course and is having some difficulty in doing his homework assignment. You sit down with him and explain some of the basic theories. You discover that you really do know what you're talking about. Tutoring is done in much the same way."
2. Ask your audience a question.
    a. "Did you ever wish you could just run away from it all?"
    b. "How many of you like apple pie?"
3. Present a quotation.
    a. "Don't try it. I've tried them all myself and they don't work." This is what my uncle always said when he first spoke to new "boots" at Great Lakes Naval Training Base.
    b. As Robert Kennedy and Martin Luther King have said, "I have a dream. Some men dream dreams and ask 'why?' I dream dreams and ask 'why not?'"
4. Refer to a historical event or date.
    a. "November 22, Dallas, Texas. John F. Kennedy, the 35th president of the United States of America lay dead; struck down by an assassin's bullet."

Grab your audience!

    b. "It was on this day in 1775 that the American Revolution began at Concord Bridge. The famous shot heard round the world had been fired."

5. Tell a joke. (Make sure it is related to your topic.)
    a. For a speech on shearing sheep you might start with, "Where do sheep get their hair cut? At baaaber shops."
    b. Suppose you are giving a speech on the importance of speaking clearly, you might start with "As a prisoner was running through the prison gates after being released, he yelled, 'I'm free, I'm free!' A child playing nearby responded, 'Big deal! I'm four!' "

6. State an unusual fact.
    a. "Ten percent of the American public are emotionally disturbed or mentally ill. That's one out of every ten people."
    b. "One of the most beautiful of all flowers, a traditional Christmas gift, has been accused of being deadly poisonous! The poinsettia's leaves can cause illness and even death!"

7. Use a gimmick (a novelty opening).
    a. Do a sleight-of-hand trick that changes a dollar bill into 35 cents to begin a speech on inflation.
    b. Have a tarantula walk up your arm to begin a speech on unusual pets.

8. Refer to the purpose of your gathering.
    a. "Five children have been injured crossing the street in front of the grade school. We must have patrolled crosswalks."
    b. "February is the month for lovers. Valentine's Day is the biggest day in the business of florists. We can sell even more flowers by advertising."

There are many ways of starting out your speech. Be creative. When preparing your introduction, just keep the three requirements in mind and try to be original and stimulating. Your speech will be off to a good start.

The Introduction Exercise

Purpose: The purpose of this exercise is to learn how to prepare a stimulating and relevant speech introduction.

Procedure:

1. Bring a short news article to class (or the instructor may hand out articles to read).

2. Referring to the eight styles of introductions listed in chapter 2, prepare an introduction for that article. Make sure it fulfills the requirements for an introduction.
   a. It should gain the audience's attention.
   b. It should tell the audience what the subject matter will be.
   c. It should tie the speaker to the audience.
3. The introduction should be 40 seconds to one minute in length.
4. The introduction may not start with, "My speech is about . . ."
5. Present the introduction orally in class or write it out and submit it to your instructor for comments.

The final step in preparing your speech for presentation is to compose a **conclusion**. Since this is the last your audience will hear from you, you will want to leave them with a clear, positive statement to remember. A conclusion should occupy about 10 percent of your allotted time. An effective conclusion must do three things.

1. A conclusion re-emphasizes the main point of your speech.
2. A conclusion climaxes your speech by tying everything together.
3. A conclusion leaves your audience remembering what you said.

Just as your introduction informs your audience of what you are going to tell them, your conclusion tells them what you have said. You should make a clear comment restating the main theme of your speech. After all, your audience will leave with some idea as to what your point was, so it should be what you intended it to be. Tell them again what you have been trying to emphasize.

Don't leave your audience hanging. Let your audience know that you are finished speaking to them. Do this in such a manner that they are prepared for your leaving the podium. Don't just walk away. Make sure you have shown them that the information you have been relating all works together to arrive at this conclusion.

And finally, conclude your speech in a manner that will make your audience remember what you want them to. You want them to remember a specific point. Don't leave them guessing.

Conclusions can be prepared in the same styles we have talked about for writing introductions. You can conclude with any of the following:

1. A question
2. A quote
3. An historical event
4. An example
5. A joke
6. An unusual fact
7. A gimmick
8. The purpose for gathering

You can also conclude your speech in one of the following ways:

1. Summarize what you have said.
   "Therefore, in summary, I'd like to remind you that there are six steps to making the best-ever chocolate cake: 1) Get your recipe, 2) Assemble your ingredients, 3) Prepare your utensils, 4) Mix, 5) Bake and 6) Eat. If you follow these instructions, you can't go wrong."

2. Give an invitation to your audience to look toward the future.
   "The year 2001 is only a few years away. We all will have a choice in determining whether it will be a world of peace and brotherhood or one of civil strife and bloodshed."

3. Call your audience to action.
   "I've told you the importance of giving blood and why the need is so great. Won't you please help yourself and your fellow man by signing up to donate blood at the March 1st blood drive?"

However you decide to conclude your speech, make sure it fits the three requirements previously mentioned. In addition, make sure that your audience is prepared for your departure from the podium. Don't just take your notes and walk back to your seat or say, "Well, that's about it." Remember the conclusion is an ending and wrapping up of the product, i.e., speech, that you have worked so hard to achieve. The thing you don't want them to remember about all your hard work is that they were confused when you left them because they didn't know you were finished with your presentation.

With a well-prepared conclusion you will be leaving your audience with a neatly packaged set of information to remember and use as needed. There will be no doubt that you have achieved your goal.

The Conclusion Exercise

Purpose: The purpose of this exercise is to learn how to prepare a speech conclusion.

Procedure:

1. Bring a short news article to class (or the instructor may hand out articles to read).
2. Referring to the different styles of conclusion in chapter 2, prepare a conclusion for that article. Make sure it fulfills the requirements for a speech conclusion:
   a. It re-emphasizes the main point of your speech.
   b. It climaxes your speech by tying everything together.
   c. It leaves your audience remembering what you said.
3. The conclusion should be forty seconds to one minute in length.
4. The conclusion may not be, "Well, that's about it . . ." or "Are there any questions?"
5. Present the conclusion in class or write it down and submit it to your instructor for comments.

Conclusion

You now know the importance of and how to be specific and organized about the speeches you will be delivering. By outlining you have determined the map for the journey through the speech, and whether you organized the material spatially, chronologically, in a process or by priority, the audience should be able to follow you. Most of our discussion in the first three chapters has dealt with topics for which you have sufficient information in your own head and experience—topics which you can treat without exhaustive research. Many speeches will, however, require a trip to the library or other outside source. We shall next cover how to make those trips successful ones.

Study Questions

1. Define specific purpose and compose three.
2. List several reasons why you should outline your speech.

3. Name four methods of ordering the material in an outline for a speech.
4. What are the three goals of an introduction?
5. Prepare five different ways of introducing the same topic and indicate the advantages of each.
6. Prepare three different ways of concluding the same speech.

Key Words

Chronological organization
Conclusion
Formal outline
Introduction
Priority organization

Process organization
Spatial organization
Specific purpose
Working outline

4 Researching the Topic

Chapter Four Outline

I. Why do you need to research your topic?
   A. You may need to find additional information.
   B. You must support your ideas.

II. You must become information literate.
   A. You must recognize when information would be useful.
   B. You must discover where information is available.
   C. You need to know how to get information.
   D. You must understand what to do with the gathered information.
   E. You must communicate the information effectively.

III. There are many sources available for researching your speech.
   A. The library isn't the only place to find sources.
   B. The library exists to provide numerous sources in one location.
       1. Librarians are knowledgeable people; ask for their assistance.
       2. Become familiar with the layout of your library.
       3. The card catalog is a good means of locating information.
       4. Reference materials offer information.
       5. Periodicals are excellent sources of recent information.
       6. Electronic research sources are available in many libraries.
   C. People are invaluable research material.
       1. Using interviews can provide answers to support your ideas.
       2. Observations can also assist in investigating your topic.
       3. Surveys can be tools for accumulating original data.

IV. Researching involves note-taking.
   A. Locate all the sources you plan on using for your speech.
   B. Choose one source to be your primary reference.
   C. Decide what pertinent information you need from your other sources.
   D. If possible gather all your sources together.
   E. It is advisable to use note cards rather than sheets of paper to record your notes.
   F. Make bibliography cards for all your sources.
   G. Make notes on each source.

V. The final step in researching is to prepare a bibliography.
   A. Order your bibliography cards.
   B. Compile the list of sources in proper form.

VI. Information must not be plagiarized.
   A. Plagiarism is stealing.
   B. Do not copy someone else's work without giving credit.

Chapter Four

Researching the Topic

Introduction

Why do I need to research and investigate my topic? Why can't I just talk about what I know? Why should I use valuable time researching when I already know what I want to say? The answers to these questions depend entirely upon the circumstances in which you give your speech. There are certainly times when you will wish to present an impromptu speech and have no research time available. Do you keep your mouth shut and not share your ideas? Of course not; you mentally collect those ideas, quickly organize them and pray you remember the information correctly. Then you deliver your speech. On the other hand, most speaking engagements will be known in advance, allowing ample time to research your specific topic.

Why Research?

The general rule of thumb for researching is this: *Make time to investigate.* Time spent learning new facts, clarifying ideas and finding examples during the research process will ultimately save you time later in the speech process. Even though you believe you're well informed about your topic, you will most likely find that you need additional information. You may need to perform an experiment and gather data, or read about a particular peace treaty; verify the wording of a law or an ingredient in Mom's sweet pickle recipe. You may need a chart, story, recording, etc., or need to give credit to your dad for teaching you how to change a flat tire. Whatever your speech is about, adding information to what you already know will help you decide what to include. With this data you may discover that some material is not as important as you thought or you hadn't included some major or interesting point.

How do you know you've done enough research? How much "support" is enough? Common sense and time limits will help you here. In a six- to eight-minute coverage on the homeless you should have enough time and should include three actual case study experiences of those suffering this condition. Place yourself in the audience's shoes. What would you like to have presented about this problem? Combine the demographic research you collected during the audience analysis process with additional information you have discovered and you will be building a well-organized and effective speech.

You will always do more research than you will ever use. This does not mean that the research was in vain. The more background you investigate, the more confident you will be at the podium, thus adding to your sense of security and easing nervousness.

Research also substantiates and supports your ideas, giving your audience reasons to believe what you say. Researching involves collecting examples, quotes, statistics and any other material that will show your audience that you know what you are talking about.

As you can see, there are many reasons to do research for your speaking engagement. It is obviously advantageous to investigate your topic with sources that add to your original ideas. The question is no longer "Should I do research?" but "How do I get started?"

There are entire courses devoted to how to research. Many of you have already taken a course that required you to do the dreaded research paper. If you have completed such a course, this section can serve as a reminder. If you haven't, this unit will give you some basic information on how to acquire the necessary research for your speeches.

Information Literacy

We no longer live in a world where we can absorb all the necessary facts, techniques, theories, etc., that we will find necessary to know throughout our lifetime. One daily edition of the *Christian Science Monitor* contains more information than people born in 1900 were expected to know in an entire lifetime. Information is doubling in less than three years time and by the year 2000 A.D., the amount of information available will most likely double in half that time. Obviously we must learn how to increase our **information literacy**. This can be done by developing and using the following research and critical thinking skills:

1. Recognize when information would be useful.
2. Discover where information is available.

3. Know how to get information.
4. Understand what to do with the gathered information.
5. Communicate the information effectively.

Research and Sources

If the first place your mind (and probably your body) wanders to when you think of researching is the library, then pay close attention. There is literally a universe of information available *outside* the library doors. The following is only a small sampling of those sources that aren't necessarily housed in the library.

Television shows, radio shows, movies
Family diaries, journals
CDs and other audio recordings
Advertisements
A class (formal/informal)
Discussions with other people
Museums
Your aunt's recipes
Aquariums
Embassies and consulate offices
Discussions over coffee with friends
AA Meetings
Churches
Civic organizations
Communication software
A talk with your grandfather
Slides, photographs, paintings, posters

Many interesting and creative approaches involve music, actual recordings of news events, quotes or vocal dramatizations. These could not be found in any other sources. It is one thing to read about a certain type of music or historical event. It is quite another thing to hear the music or listen to the announcer as they describe the actual event as it took place. Non-printed materials will also provide you with many supplements to your speech to use as audio-visual aids. Don't limit your search to the library, go exploring.

Now that you realize that the library doesn't have to be the first and only stop on your information hunt, it's time to look at the sources and advantages that a library provides. After all, the only real reason for a library to exist is to provide numerous sources at one convenient location. Libraries are very user-friendly once you are acquainted with some general sources. Later you can expand upon these basic materials.

Librarians are knowledgeable people, and are there to assist you with your research. If you don't know where to start or are having difficulties, ask your librarians. They can be invaluable aids to investigation. However, don't expect them to do your research for you. That's your job. Use their knowledge just as you would any other source, and if they gave you specific information on your topic, be sure to include their names in your list of sources.

Researching is easier if you are familiar with the facilities you will be using. Most libraries offer an orientation or tour of their holdings. If your school offers such help, it would be wise to take advantage of the opportunity. You will be surprised at the different sources available. Every library is different, but this next section lists the most commonly used sources and suggests directions for further research aids.

Card Catalog

The **card catalog** is one of the most familiar and well-used sources in the library. The card catalog in your library may be still set up in a large cabinet of small drawers that occupies a space near the entrance. More likely you will find that it has been replaced by an on-line computer or is on microfiche. You will find all the books your library has available in alphabetical order listed in this location. Most card catalogs are divided into three sections according to subject, author and title. If you know the title of a book, you would look under the title section. If you know the name of an author, check under the name. Usually, you will find that looking under the subject heading will be the easiest and quickest way to use the card catalog. Once you've found the books you believe you need, look at the numbers and letters in the top left corner of the card or data entry. They refer to the system of organizing material that your library uses. Most libraries today use the Library of Congress System, but you may find that your library is still organized under the Dewey Decimal system. Either way, these numbers show you the location of your book. You can locate the section your book is in, by matching the letters and numbers from the card to the corresponding notation on the book shelves.

Reference Works

Reference works are materials such as encyclopedias, *The World Almanac, Who's Who in America*, dictionaries and other texts that include information about specific topics. These will be

*Explore specific reference works in various disciplines:
science, medicine, automechanics, literature, etc.*

listed in the card catalog and may be found the same way you found
other books. Another way of locating these sources is to look for
the reference section in your library and just browse. Browsing is
probably the best since you will most likely not be familiar with
all the different reference works. Look around and you will be
surprised at the different sources you can find.

A word of caution is appropriate about using encyclopedias. Don't
use them as your only source. These volumes are very familiar to
most of us. We've all used them as our primary resource for many
oral reports. They are excellent sources of basic knowledge, but
when you are preparing a specific speech topic you should not limit
your investigation to using only encyclopedias. Often the article in
the encyclopedia will include, at the end, a list of additional sources
to check. Be brave! You will find that there is more timely and
extensive information in other reference volumes.

Books and encyclopedias are excellent sources of basic general
knowledge, but you should be aware that because of the time it
takes to publish any given book, the information contained therein

is probably one to two years old, regardless of the copyright date. Do not assume that just because you have a book on abortion, you have all the current, up-to-the-minute information on that topic. To find the most current material, periodicals are your best source.

Periodicals

Periodicals are magazines, newspapers and journals. These will usually be located in a specific section of the library devoted only to them. You will also find that many of these works (particularly newspapers) have been transferred to microfilm and must be read on a special viewer. If this is the case with the information you need, consult the librarian for assistance in using the machine. To find particular articles about your topic you will want to refer to the many different abstracts and indexes that have categorized these areas. For popular magazines you will probably use *The Readers' Guide to Periodical Literature*. For more specific, specialized areas you will have to look at other indexes that contain references to your topic. Most national professional journals are titled *The Journal of the American . . .* , *The American . . .* , or *National Society of . . .* , so remember to look under National, American or Journal when using an index to search for sources in various indexes. The best way to use these guides is to look under several general headings that may contain your topic. Locate articles that relate to your topic and look them up.

Computerization

There have been enormous advances made in computer software and other **electronic research sources** in very recent history. As a matter of fact, advances are being made so rapidly that it is impossible to give a current list of all that is available. These sources allow you to do your research more efficiently than ever before. They are faster and less redundant than traditional sources and should be taken advantage of. The best advice is to ask your librarian what is available and then jump in and learn how to use the computer. You'll soon find yourself spending less time and accomplishing more when your research takes you to the library. The following is a short list of a variety of electronic research sources that your library may have.

There are many computerized catalogs and indexes for specific interest areas: *Editorials on File*, *ERIC* (education), *PsycLit* (psychology), *SIRS*, etc. CD ROM technology has provided a means

*Electronic research sources make research quicker
and easier than ever before.*

to make encyclopedias, almanacs and indexes available in a most efficient way. Information stored on CD ROM is similar to the discs you play on your personal CD or laser disc player. These discs contain information that can be pulled up on a computer screen and read but not erased. The *Wilson Disc* is essentially the same source as the bound *Readers' Guide to Periodical Literature* which lists articles in common periodicals by subject. Use of this resource will not only make things quicker and easier to find but also help you sort through the information to more accurately pinpoint which articles cover your topic best. Ask your librarian if these sources are available in your library.

Two other suggestions before we move on may be of use. (1) Don't limit yourself to the use of one library. Unless you live in an isolated area you should have access to several libraries. Even if you can't check out materials from a particular library due to residency requirements you can still probably use them to do in-house research. (2) For the growing number of PC owners who have modems and can access information on-line from their own homes, there are many services that provide immediate entrance to several sources of information including electronic encyclopedias. (Note: This service usually carries a fee in addition to telephone line use.) Take yourself on a scavenger hunt and find out what's available.

Library Search

Purpose: To give the student experience with the various reference sources in the library.

Procedure: Check the reference sources in the library for answers to the following questions. Try finding them yourself without the help of the librarian.

1. Find the date of the first performance of Bizet's *Carmen*.
2. Does your library have an individual copy of Shakespeare's *Twelfth Night*?
3. Find a statistic on the number of homeless in the city of New York.
4. Find the 1987 "stats" for St. Louis Cardinal John Tudor.
5. Who was Isak Dinesen?
6. Where is the Jutland Peninsula located?
7. Who was Felix Frankfurter?
8. Find three symbols used in hieroglyphics.
9. What does a minaret look like?
10. Where is the Eiffel Tower located?
11. How many abortions were performed in the U.S. in 1987?
12. Does your library have a recording of the Beatles singing "Yesterday"?
13. What does "mellifluous" mean?
14. What did "large" mean in 1688?
15. What did the word "bitch" mean in 1675 and what does it mean now?
16. What three famous songs did Irving Berlin write?
17. Find the titles of three operas written by Mozart.
18. What religious sculpture piece is Michelangelo famous for?
19. Where does the Pablo Picasso painting *Woman with Fan* hang?
20. How many anthologies in your library have the Robert Frost poem "Wild Grapes"?

Methods of Research

Most beginning speakers tend to limit their research to what they can find in the library or from personal experience. Doing this not only eliminates several other possible sources, but it also fails to use the most interesting and creative aspects of investigation—other people. Real live people are often much more interesting and informative than any written volumes that are usually not as up-to-date as first-hand knowledge.

Interviews

Interviewing is a research method whereby you question people who are knowledgeable in your field of research and record their answers. This allows you to take advantage of experts. If you know, or know of, someone who has experience or a background on your topic, by all means go talk to them. Don't just stop by their office or stop them in the hall. Make an appointment. When you make the appointment, tell them what it is you are interested in and then be sure to be on time. It is also important that you know what information you want them to give you. Don't go into the interview

Interviews can be a part of research.

and say, "Tell me what you know about gardening." Rather, tell them what your specific purpose is and ask questions that relate directly to your goal. It is a good idea to write down any questions that you want to ask before you go to the appointment. That way you will not waste anyone's time and will be well organized. Make notes on what is said or ask permission to tape the conversation. Be sure to thank the person for the interview and give them credit as one of your sources in your speech and outline.

Interview

Purpose: This exercise will give you "hands on" experience with the interviewing techniques discussed in the chapter. You may also use it to support your topic for a speech.

Procedure: Choose a topic which would benefit from personal interview support material. Pick a person who is knowledgeable in this area.

1. Make an appointment to see this person.
2. Develop questions (probably 4 or 5) which you can ask.
3. Interview your subject.
4. Write a simple "thank you" note to this person.

Observations

Observation—watching behavior and recording a pattern to that behavior—can also be a way of investigating your topic. Watching behaviors can help support certain stands given in your speech. Vague, general observations are not very useful in supporting data, but well-designed studies on specific occurrences can add to your research.

Decide what you need to observe. What type of behaviors are observed? Where can you easily do your observing without being in the way? Make sure any conclusions you draw from such observations are typical and not due to any unusual circumstances.

Surveys

Surveys are another type of investigation that can be used in research. **Surveys** are questions asked to groups of people to gather information and may request factual data or ask for opinions. There are basically two types of surveys: (1) written questionnaires and (2) verbal surveys.

Questionnaires ask the person responding to give answers on specific topics. The form should also include general demographic information about the person answering, such as age, occupation, gender and any other information pertinent to assign your answers to categories. Verbal surveys should include the same kinds of information; the main difference is that instead of requesting written statements, you receive verbal responses. In other words, you ask people questions and they answer you orally. This can be accomplished in direct person-to-person contact or over the telephone.

Survey questions can be written in many different ways, depending on your purpose in asking the question. You may want to ask questions that require only a "yes" or "no" answer, or give the responder a choice of a few multiple answers. These types of surveys work well when you are trying to find out specific factual data, are interested in tabulations of numbers, or have limited time to get responses. If you are primarily interested in opinions, you would be better off using open-ended questions. Open-ended questions are questions that require the person responding to give the most information, to expand their response from a simple "yes" or "no" to more detailed data. Asking people to explain why they believe as they do or to cite examples are ways of using open-ended questions. Surveys take time to prepare, distribute and tabulate, but they are some of the best sources of current information that you will be able to find and essential if you need to know what people are thinking.

There are probably infinite references for any one speech and a well-researched speech will be much more substantial and effective than one which is put together without outside sources. Caution, however, should be taken when you are looking for sources for your speech. It is better to locate a few good references than it is to overload yourself with many superfluous ones. Find three or four sources and use them rather than getting bogged down with so many that you have neither the time, nor the space to use them all.

Making Research Notes

Researching involves note-taking. Once you have located the sources you will use, you must have a way of recording the information you plan on using. This is true whether your material comes from printed sources, interviews or any other media.

Note-taking is a very important skill that can be learned. Many of you are already proficient in this skill. You may have already developed your own style—something that works well for you. If this is true, then the following information should not affect your current method. If, however, you find yourself at a loss on what notes to take, have difficulty in organizing your notes or problems in deciphering what you've written, then the following suggestions will help you become a more efficient note-taker. Notice that the type of notes we are talking about in this section are *not* the notes you will be taking with you to the podium. This method of note-taking is for your research work.

There are nine steps to taking good notes.

1. *Locate all the sources you plan on using for your speech.* Knowing what is available will help you decide what percentage of each source you want to rely on for information. If you find there are numerous references for your topic, you will want to look over them quickly, keeping only the most comprehensive or up-to-date sources. An over-abundance of books, articles, etc. will only complicate your research. If there are few sources on your topic you may wish to check other possible sources, choose a different topic, or rely heavily on two or three sources. Once you have located only those sources you will actually use for information, it is time to move on to the next step.

2. *Choose one source to be your primary reference.* Use the source that you believe is the most basic and comprehensive as your primary source of information. The notes on this reference will be the most complete.

3. *Decide what pertinent information you need from your other sources.* Since you will be taking basic information from the previously discussed source, your other materials must do one or more of the following:
   a. Provide additional support for a view in your primary source.
   b. Fill in missing information from the general view.
   c. Give a more detailed account than the comprehensive source.
   d. Approach the information in a creative or novel way.
   e. Illustrate your topic with audio/visual aids.

4. *If possible, gather all your sources together.* If it is possible to have all your sources available in one spot, do so. This will save time and be less confusing.

5. *It is advisable to use note cards rather than sheets of paper to record your notes.* Using note cards (ruled or unruled, any

size) will enable you to categorize your various bits of information easier than searching through sheets of notebook paper. Each note card can be labeled by the information on it and later, after all the notes are taken, they can be divided into categories.

6. *Make bibliography cards for all your sources.* For each source, make a separate card with the information necessary to record it as a source. (Standard bibliography form is covered in the next section of this chapter.) When you have recorded all your sources, label each source with a capital letter in the upper right section of the card. Your first source would be "A," your second "B," etc.

Example:

A

Campbell, Mary. *Teach Yourself WordPerfect 5.1.*
St. Louis: Osborne McGraw-Hill, 1990.

---

7. *Make notes on each source.* You are now ready to begin taking notes on your topic. Each note card should be labeled by the capital letter assigned to the reference it is taken from and numbered chronologically, i.e., the first card from source "A" would be marked "A1," the second "A2," etc. By labeling your notes, you will know what source they are from and in what order they were recorded in your source. Give each note a heading, describing what the information on the card is about. For instance, if the information is on historical background,

a quote or statistics about a certain study, label it as such. Put only information about that heading on that card. Do not combine information or it will be difficult to sort out later.

Example:

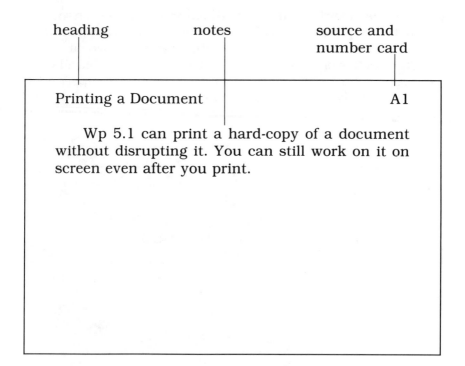

heading   notes   source and
                                            number card

Printing a Document   A1

   Wp 5.1 can print a hard-copy of a document without disrupting it. You can still work on it on screen even after you print.

Notes on the card may be direct quotes or paraphrases from your source. These notes may be written in complete sentences or phrases; it doesn't matter as long as you can understand them when you read them several days later. Take notes on anything you think you will need to illustrate, explain or support your topic. Be aware of your focused topic and time limit so you don't compile more information than you can cover.

Now that all your research has been completed, you should write your outline. You are then ready to complete the bibliography.

How to Prepare a Bibliography

The last step in the research speech preparation is the preparing of the bibliography. If your research and note-taking have been done accurately, you should have no trouble with this step.

Organize your Bibliography Cards. Because your **bibliography** will be a list of the sources you used to prepare this speech, all you need to do is alphabetize the cards you have made of your sources. If you have done interviews, you should make a card for them as well. Some bibliographies are separated into "printed" and "non-printed" sources. Check with your instructor about the form he or she requires. The alphabetizing occurs by the last name of the author or the first significant word of the title (if no author is given), and the last name of the interviewed party.

Compile the List. The form for bibliographies is standard and the bibliography should follow the conclusion section of your formal outline.

It is necessary that you give credit to any source you used in the preparation of your speech. The following information will show the standard procedure for listing the most frequently used sources. Should you need to include any other type of reference, please refer to any standard text on writing a paper. Your English faculty will be a good source to tap.

Items in a bibliography are listed alphabetically by the authors' names or the name of the person interviewed with reversed indentation.

Books:
> Macleod, Charlotte. *The Resurrection Man.* New York: Warner Books, Inc. 1992.

Encyclopedias:
> *McGraw-Hill Encyclopedia of Science and Technology*, 6th edition. New York: McGraw-Hill, 1987.

Newspaper Articles:
> Weller, Linda N. "Edwardsville Seniors Don't Have a Prayer," *The Alton Telegraph*, 11 May 1993, A. p. 1.

Magazine Articles:
> Meers, Trevor. "Clearing The Confusion of Software Categories." *PC NOVICE*, May 1993, pp. 30–33.

Pamphlets:
> *Summer Programs 1993*. Girl Scouts, Land of Lincoln Council, April 1993.

Audio Recordings:
> Beethoven, Ludwig van, *Symphony #1*, The Hanover Band, NI 5003, Nimbus Records, Ltd., 1983.

Films:
>   *Beauty and the Beast*. Directed by Gary Trousdale and Kirk
>   Wise. Walt Disney Home Video, 1991.

Television Programs:
>   *Home Improvement*. ABC, 12 May 1993.

Interviews:
>   Drayer, Betty J. Interview. Professor of History, Lewis and Clark
>   Community College. Godfrey, IL, 15 May, 1993.

Personal Experiences:
>   Your name (last name first). List experience relevant to topic.
>   Home address.

A Word about Plagiarism

Students often find themselves in trouble when they present research information in oral or written form due to plagiarism. **Plagiarism** is, most simply, stealing. Sometimes students get into a bind and deliberately copy someone else's work and present it as their own. More often, the plagiarism occurs because he or she is not exactly sure how to present the data that has been gathered. He or she then either directly uses the author's exact words (verbatim) without attributing the quote to the source, or paraphrases some of the words but repeats all the main ideas without giving credit. Avoid this serious problem by citing all your sources and indicating when you are quoting verbatim. If you are in doubt about whether you are plagiarizing, speak to your instructor. Never take credit for something that isn't your own work.

Conclusion

Having researched your material, you will be certain that you have a firm foundation for your statements. The audience will have reason to believe what you are saying because you can support your data. These factors will give you the extra confidence needed to know that your speech is well prepared. Now you can move on to the second important aspect of giving a speech—your delivery.

Study Questions

1. Name four sources not found in the library available for researching your topic.
2. Name four sources found in the library.
3. What types of electronic research sources are available in your library?
4. What is a bibliography?
5. How do surveys or questionnaires help support your information?
6. Describe the process for finding a magazine article in the library using the *Wilson Disk* or the *Readers' Guide to Periodical Literature.*
7. Choose a topic and list several research sources you would use.
8. Why are books not always the most current, up-to-date source?
9. List three things to do to conduct an effective interview.

Key Words

Bibliography
Card catalog
Electronic research
  sources
Information literacy
Interview

Observation
Periodicals
Plagiarism
Reference works
Surveys

5

Delivery

Chapter Five Outline

Part I—Verbal Delivery

  I. As a speaker you are dependent upon the sound your voice produces.
     A. Sound production depends upon the lungs and diaphragm.
     B. Sound production depends upon the larynx, mouth and head.
     C. There are exercises you can use to produce a pleasant vocal quality.

  II. Sound must be used effectively.
     A. Rate is the speed at which words are delivered.
     B. Volume refers to the loudness of tone.
     C. Pitch is the placement of sound on a musical scale.
     D. Tone combines rate, volume and pitch to produce the desired emotional response from the audience.

  III. A smooth delivery relies on verbal elements.
     A. The audience must understand the meaning of the words used.
     B. Standard grammar must be used.
     C. Words must be properly pronounced and enunciated.
     D. Transitions should be varied to lead from point to point.

Part II—Nonverbal Delivery

  I. A smooth delivery depends upon nonverbal elements.
     A. Establishing eye contact with the audience is important.
     B. Good podium posture is essential.
     C. Proper use of gestures adds interest to the speech.
     D. Facial expressions show your audience how you feel about the topic.
     E. Appearance helps set the mood before you begin to speak.

  II. Audio/Visual aids should be used to help the speaker's presentation.
     A. Visual presentations must follow three rules.
       1. They must be large enough to be seen by all.
       2. They should be controllable.
       3. They must be pertinent to the topic.
     B. Audio presentations must follow three guidelines.
       1. They must be clear and easy to hear.
       2. They must be controllable.
       3. They should be pertinent to the topic.
     C. You may need to use special equipment or people as props.

III. It is important to practice your speech aloud before you present it to your audience.
   A. You must rehearse your speech several times.
   B. Practicing is necessary for several reasons.
      1. You must time your presentation.
      2. You must practice verbal elements.
      3. You must observe nonverbal aspects of your speaking.
   C. You can get feedback from your rehearsal in many ways.
      1. Present the speech to a person.
      2. Use a tape recorder.
      3. Use a camcorder.
      4. Watch yourself in a full-length mirror.
IV. The notes you take to the podium are very important.
   A. Make them simple.
   B. Have them ordered.
   C. Make them brief.

Chapter Five

Delivery

Introduction

After all the preparation you've done for your speech, you probably believe that you are ready to present it to your audience. This might be true if you were preparing a *written* theme or report, but you are only half-way home when it comes to making speeches. All the researching and organizing has prepared you to know what you are going to say and is important to your final outcome, but *making a speech is essentially a performance.* After all, a speech is given to an audience for a specific reason. This audience will not be reading what you have to say; they will be hearing and watching you. You may have done an excellent job of researching and organizing your content material, but if your performance is poor, none of that will matter. Your job is one of conveying that information to your audience.

A performance involves verbal and nonverbal elements necessary to carry your viewpoint to your audience. The process of presenting your information to an audience is called **delivery**. A practiced, smooth delivery is vital to a successful speech.

Assuming you've done a good job in researching and organizing your material, you are now ready to begin working on the finished product—the actual delivery of your speech. All the work you have already done should assure you that you know about the topic you will be covering, and that your subject matter will flow in a logical, easy-to-follow pattern. This is the **content** of your speech, the information it contains. Now you must make sure your audience will receive that information in a clear and understandable way. A good delivery involves many aspects of verbal and nonverbal behavior. We will examine each behavior individually, but remember, they must all work together to produce a polished performance.

Sound Production

Because your performance as a speaker is highly dependent upon vocal delivery, it is time to take an in-depth view of how the sound of your voice is produced. Ultimately, the success of any public speaking event is judged on the actual presentation of that speech to a particular audience. Audience analysis, focusing, research and organization will have helped, but the true test of an effective speaker is how he or she handles the actual delivery.

Lungs and Diaphragm

The sound of your voice is produced from air which has been stored in your lungs. The capacity of the lungs is determined not only by how much you jog or smoke, but by a thin membrane which stretches from your solar plexus, under the lungs and rib cage to your spine; the **diaphragm**. This membrane is often one of the first areas of your body that is attacked by stage fright. Like any muscle under stress it tends to shrink, diminishing the potential air supply of your lungs. To illustrate the process of air movement in your body as it is controlled by the diaphragm, perform the following exercise:

Balloon Exercise

To appreciate more fully the membrane called the diaphragm, get an ordinary balloon. Uninflated, the balloon's texture resembles the diaphragm itself without stage fright; it is resilient and pliable, yet remarkably strong (unless attacked with a pin or sharp object). (Remember this membrane lies beneath the lungs and controls the volume of air permitted in the lungs.) Now blow up the balloon. As you perform this simple task of transferring air from your lungs to the balloon, notice how often you need to take a new breath to blow. Does the exchange of air in your lungs (i.e., inhale and exhale) take five to seven seconds or longer? Or are you more rapidly blowing up the balloon? The shorter the time for a complete breath (inhaling and exhaling), the shallower you are probably breathing, and the less lung capacity or potential you are using. The inflated balloon resembles the texture of the diaphragm with stage fright—not so much give. By this exercise you have seen two things: the texture of the diaphragm and the capacity of your lungs.

Because air (in the form of breath) is the primary source of the sounds we make, let's look at the breathing process. To produce sounds successfully we must know how to regulate and control the

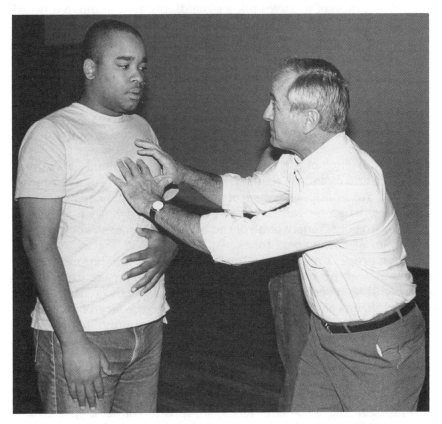

Proper breathing techniques are important.

air flow. Here's the process. When we breathe, the following physical actions occur:

1. The muscles of the diaphragm tense, contract and move downward becoming more flat than domed.
2. This descending movement of the diaphragm compresses the stomach, liver and kidneys which causes a bulge in the abdominal walls.
3. The rib cage raises up and outward.

The preceding procedure causes the air pressure in the lungs to decrease, creating a partial vacuum so that air from outside rushes in to equalize the pressure.

As we reverse the process and exhale, the procedure reverses itself.

1. Relaxation of muscles allows the diaphragm to move upward (or we may constrict the diaphragm forcing air out of the lungs.)
2. The stomach, liver and kidneys return to their uncompressed positions.
3. The ribs then move down and inward due to the pull of gravity.

All the above actions cause a decrease in the size of the chest cavity which compresses the air in the lungs. This means that the air pressure in the lungs is now greater than the pressure outside the body and air is expelled through the mouth and nose.

In the absence of any physical respiratory problems, breathing (inhaling and exhaling) requires no conscious control or awareness. It is an automatic response of our body which keeps us alive. However, when we talk, we must be aware of what we are doing in order to consciously control the breathing process and produce effective, pleasing vocal tones.

When proper breathing techniques are used, inhalations are less frequent and the speaker will not have to gasp for breath because there will be a reserve of air. Longer phrases can be uttered and jerky rhythms can be avoided. Furthermore, the larynx and throat will be less tense which will improve vocal quality.

Correcting Extreme Upper-Chest Breathing

Purpose: The purpose of this exercise is to correct a speaker's shallow breathing that can interfere with effective speaking patterns.

Procedure:

1. Lie with your back flat on the floor. Place a book or pillow under your head which will raise the head 3/4 to 1 inch. This places the head in the proper position for normal breathing.
2. Put your right hand on your abdomen and your left hand on the upper part of your chest above your sternum. Breathe as naturally as possible, inhale through the nose and exhale through the mouth or nose. Notice the expansion and contraction that occurs under your right hand and the little movement under your left hand. When you are aware of these movements, stand up and breathe in the same manner. Be careful not to lift your shoulders.

The Larynx

Air from the lungs passes through the windpipe and into the **larynx** (located at the top of the esophagus) which contains two membranes sometimes called "vocal cords." As the air passes over the larynx, sounds are produced, tones which we call "vocal pitch," much as a harmonica vibrates and produces a tone when we blow or suck on it. Certain instruments of the orchestra also produce sounds from the concentration of air on their reeds or mouthpieces. Therefore, your voice (sound from the larynx) is dependent upon free access to the air from your lungs.

The Mouth and Head

Having produced the sound with your larynx, you must then project that sound to the ear of your listener. Your mouth and head cavities perform much the same function as the electric amplifier in a band: the mouth concentrates the sound into words, and the cavities of the sinuses and head provide "sound chambers" to further refine and enhance the sound as it leaves your body.

Hence, lungs, larynx and mouth all combine in a complex process which is so commonplace, you produce sound without even thinking of it. Sometimes our lack of attention to the production of sound can lead to poor or harsh vocal qualities which may distract our listeners. Here are some exercises you can try to improve both the relaxation of the muscles of vocal production and the quality of sound produced.

Relaxation Exercise

Purpose: Since the voice may appear "tight" or strident at any time stress is apparent, the purpose of this exercise is to develop a means of quick relaxation that can be learned easily and used frequently as the speaker feels the need.

Procedure:
1. Close your eyes and picture yourself in that one spot where you are most comfortable and relaxed.
2. Try to recall how you feel physically, mentally and emotionally when you are at that spot. Let the tension (and with it stage fright) drain away as you concentrate on your favorite spot.
3. Now slowly bring yourself back to the present and actual surroundings. Open your eyes as you maintain those relaxed muscles and calm thoughts.

Yawning Exercise

Purpose: The purpose of this exercise is to give the speaker an experiment to feel the relaxation in the throat that will keep the voice from sounding tense.

Procedure:

1. Rest your tongue on the floor of your mouth and yawn.
2. Repeat several times. This will result in a reasonably relaxed throat.
3. Say "ah" continuing the sound for about five seconds. Don't let any tightness or tension enter your throat. If your throat begins to tense, discontinue the sound and repeat the yawn before attempting to vocalize again.
4. When you can sustain the sound for five seconds or more without tension, try the exercise by vocalizing each of the following sounds: oo, ee, uh, ou, oh.

Alphabet Exercise

Purpose: The purpose of this exercise is to allow the speaker to determine if voice support is sufficient or if air is escaping unnecessarily.

Procedure:

1. Take a deep breath.
2. Without hurrying too much, try to say the alphabet in one breath. If you can't make it all the way through you aren't breathing correctly. Don't strain. Relax. Easy does it.

Building Loudness

Purpose: The purpose of this exercise is to increase a speaker's volume by learning how to avoid excess air release.

Procedure:

1. Whisper the sound "ah."
2. Repeat the sound as you gradually build the volume but avoid "breathiness." Remember to breathe deeply and tense those inner throat muscles to keep the unvoiced airflow from leaking out.

What to Do with the Sound Once It Is Produced: Techniques for Variety and Clarity

Remembering that effective speakers make their speeches understandable and interesting to their audience, the following areas should be understood and used effectively to gain the greatest benefits from the sound you are producing.

Rate

Rate refers to the speed or rapidity of delivery of words. The audience will be aware of an increase in rate as a speaker becomes "caught up" in his or her speech. They will listen with a heightened sense of urgency as the speaker reaches the climax. Also, rate can be used to good effect if you are telling stories, reading drama cuttings, or delivering stand-up comedy. You can distinguish between characters with rate alone—no need for pitch or volume. Take, for example, the delightful scene in *Alice in Wonderland* when Alice meets the caterpillar. He, as you remember, is seated on top of a mushroom, smoking a water pipe (a remarkably contemporary pastime). Alice, who is now just three inches tall, peeks over the mushroom and addresses the caterpillar. (Just for fun, try reading this selection with only a change in rate to differentiate the characters. Read the caterpillar, because he's high, at just half the speed of Alice.)

Caterpillar: "Whoooo are yooooo?"

Alice: "I'm not quite sure, Sir. You see, I was Alice when I got up this morning, but I've been changed several times since then."

Caterpillar: "What do you mean by that? Explain yourself."

Alice: "Well, I can't explain myself, because I'm, not myself, you see."

Caterpillar: "I *don't* see."

Alice: "And being all these sizes in one day is confusing."

Caterpillar: "It isn't."

Alice: "It isn't what?"

Caterpillar: "It isn't confusing."

Alice: "Well, perhaps your feelings make it different. All I know is it's very queer to me."

Caterpillar: "You? Whoooo are yooooou?"

—Lewis Carroll, *Alice's Adventures in Wonderland*

Notice the long O's. These sections could be expanded almost to the point of singing them to produce the effect of a caterpillar high on drugs. And whether you are male or female, you can distinguish between the characters by rate alone.

Take another example. You are buying a new car or a computer—something that will mean a large investment. As the salesperson winds up her pitch and you are not quite sure, what is the rate you use to say, ''Well, I'm not quite sure''? It's as if the words are being dragged out of you one by one. Note the conversations you witness daily and be aware of the speed at which certain friends share information and gossip. When you're excited, happy or sad, you use different rates. The same is true at the podium. Choose an appropriate rate to indicate your mood to the audience. Rate can be an excellent way to reveal the emotional content of your speech to an audience.

Volume

Volume refers to the relative loudness of your voice. This is similar to your sound system or television volume control at home. However, hearing your CDs is different from hearing your own voice as you are speaking. This is because your voice resonates in your sinus cavities. Usually, this difference in ''hearing'' causes you no problems, but if your sinus cavities are blocked, your voice may sound like it is booming when it is actually barely audible. Your instructor can provide you with some exercises if you feel your volume is not adequate for the audience and room you are using for your speaking.

Pitch

The term **pitch** refers to the placement of the voice on a musical scale. Even though some of you may not consider yourselves ''musical,'' you all create sounds which may be placed upon an oscilloscope and evaluated for relative ''highness'' or ''lowness''— the pitch of your voice.

Two cautions are in order—one for each sex. Men, do not attempt to force your voice into a lower register than is comfortable in an attempt to sound ''super macho.'' You may end up with a sound like the rumble of a badly-tuned automobile. And women, guard against the tendency to raise your pitch (particularly when you are presenting the emotion of excitement) to a level that is too high and nasal to be comfortable for either you or your listeners.

Most speaking is done in a "middle" register, containing and varying about three or four notes on a musical scale. But your audience would grow bored listening to just those few pitches. Most people possess a vocal range of at least an octave (eight pitches with their intermediate half-steps). With this wonderful variety available to us, why do we use only two or three? *Laziness.* We have just never tried to find what our pitch variations are and hence do not know them. Here again, your instructor can provide you with exercises which will show you your **register**—that range within which it is easy for you to speak.

Tone or Mood

The elements of rate, volume and pitch combine to produce what we'll call **tone**—the emotional quality you wish to share with your audience. If you are telling a story to support your points in a speech, you will want to give the audience all the enjoyment possible by matching the tone to the subject matter. We have all seen dramatic speakers who could move us to tears merely by the variations in their voice. Without going too deeply into this discussion, let us offer a good suggestion for the tone of your speech: *Keep the energy level high to make the talk interesting to your audience. Your enthusiasm will go a long way to bring an audience to your point of view.*

Other Verbal Elements

Although we have covered the vocal production and the ways to produce variety in the delivery, we must also consider some other areas of verbal delivery.

Semantics

Semantics is the study of the meaning of words. Any speaker must be aware of how he is phrasing his information. Just because everyone in your audience speaks English does not guarantee that the audience will understand what you are saying. We tend to think that the words we use mean the same things to everyone. Unfortunately, this is not true. Sometimes we use slang terms that are understandable only to those who use them in the same way. Even if you are using the dictionary definition of a word, you cannot be sure everyone will know what you mean. Dictionaries carry several definitions for even the simplest words. *The best rule to follow is to choose words that are commonly used in a particular way.* Any time you use a technical term or one which could be misunderstood, include a definition for the term in your speech. By doing this you will avoid the possible confusion that can occur when people have different meanings for the same word.

There are several other considerations when choosing the language for your speech. Not only must you define unfamiliar or confusing terms, but you must be aware of the possible effect certain words might have on your audience. *Words are only symbols for objects and ideas.* In logical, rational thoughts we know that words aren't really the same as the idea they symbolize. But in many cases, we do allow words to affect our emotional reactions. *Language is how we convey our thoughts, opinions and feelings.* People do react as if the words themselves are the action or feeling instead of the symbol for the deed. Keeping this in mind will help you relate to your audience. Do not use words that convey racial or ethnic slurs. Be aware of the reaction people have to what has been labeled foul or offensive language. Take into consideration any terms or phrases that might be interpreted as sexist. Being aware of the effect your words can have on your audience will help eliminate the possible production of a defensive climate.

Finally, choose your language and vocabulary so that you strike a happy medium with your audience. You do not want to talk above their heads, thus losing their understanding and interest. Be sure, also, not to talk down to them, treating them like uninformed children. Language is an important tool. Without it we would find it difficult to convey our messages. Use it wisely.

Grammar

Grammar is the system of word structure and word arrangement for a language. Using the proper grammar in presenting your speech will make your speech clearer to your audience and increase your position of authority. Remember that speech making is a formalized presentation and, therefore, standard English should be used.

All languages have dialects or regional usage of words and phrases that are commonly used and accepted by people of that specific geographic region. For example, the phrases "I seen" and "I come" are often used in the southern midwest of the United States instead of the proper usage "I saw" and "I came." While these phrases may be understandable to your audience, they are not proper English grammar and should not be used when delivering your speech. Using the right tenses of verbs and speaking in complete sentences will enhance not only the delivery but the ultimate outcome of your speech as well.

Pronunciation and Enunciation

To achieve the correct **pronunciation** of a word, you must separate and accent the syllables in the accepted manner. How often have you listened to a speaker who did not? The words are yours when you speak, and to get your message across, they should be pronounced correctly. If you have difficult or technical terms, check them with an authority on your campus or in your town. Better yet, look them up and use the diacritical markings provided in the dictionary.

Commonly Mispronounced Words

aluminum (ah-LUM-in-um)
anonymous (ah-NON-ee-muss)
athlete (ATH-leet)
athletics (ath-LET-iks)
autopsy (AW-top-see)
banquet (BAN-kuit)
Beethoven (BAY-toe-vin)
blase (blah-zay)
brochure (bro-SHUR)
cache (kash)
chagrin (sha-GRIN)
chasm (KA-zum)
chef (shef)
chic (sheek)
Chopin (SHO-pan)
comparable (KOM-pra-bull)
disastrous (diz-AA-struss)
drama (DRAH-ma)
electoral (eh-LEC-tore-all)
elite (ee-LEET)
epitome (ee-PIT-o-mee)
escape (es-KAPE)
etc. (et-SET-er-a)
facade (fah-SOD)
faux pas (FAW-PAH)
fungi (FUN-GUY)

genuine (JEN-u-in)
heir (air)
homage (OHM-aj)
hysteria (hi-STARE-i-ah)
impotent (IMP-o-tent)
indict (in-DEYET)
infamous (IN-fa-muss)
Italian (it-AL-ee-in)
lingerie (LON-jer-ee)
mischievous (MISS-chi-vuss)
often (OFF-en)
picture (PICK-tour)
pitcher (PIT-sure)
poignant (POYN-yant)
police (poe-LEESS)
precocious (pree-KO-shuss)
preferable (PREFF-er-a-bull)
probably (PRAH-bab-lee)
recognize (reh-cog-NIZE)
statistics (sta-TI-sticks)
subtle (SAH-till)
sword (sord)
theater (THEE-a-ter)
vehement (VEE-a-mint)
virile (VEER-ill)
Worcestershire (WUSS-ter-sure)

Enunciation

Enunciation refers to the pronunciation of individual vowel and consonant sounds. If you have a problem, your instructor can help with individual deficiencies here. Just be clear in your diction and your words will probably be understandable to your audience.

Transition

Transition is a means of shifting the audience's frame of reference from one idea to another. This is used when you are moving to another subject, so they can follow your organization. Often beginning speakers fall into a habit of using only the conjunction "and." In moving from one point to another in your speech there are many other connecting phrases you can use, many of which will show the relationship of the elements of your speech. Here is a small list:

on the other hand	as a result	consequently
in addition	in comparison	you've heard it said
in other words	for example	some think
however	in particular	but I suggest
we might overlook	furthermore	Let's look at it
first . . . second . . .	another reason	another way

One way of breaking out of the "and" box would be to write creative transitions right in the margin of your outline. When you then take this outline to the podium, you only need a quick glance to move smoothly and meaningfully from one segment of the speech to another.

Nonverbal Elements of Delivery

In addition to the verbal elements of the delivery the speaker must be aware of what he or she is "saying" nonverbally, with body language. Here we have included the areas of eye contact, posture, gestures, facial expressions and over-all appearance which can produce pit-falls that often diminish early podium performances.

Eye Contact

Eye contact is looking directly into the eyes of another person. Establishing eye contact with your audience is very important. The speaker who looks at his audience maintains their interest more easily and can pick up on their feedback. Both of these advantages are vital to your purpose, which is getting your message across.

Look at your audience. Look at *each* person. All too often we pick out a friendly face and ignore the others present. In classroom situations speakers zero in on the instructor, never looking at the majority of the audience. Some people stare out the window or door. Others concentrate on looking at their notes or visual aids. *The impressive speaker looks at each member of the audience, individually and as a group.* In doing so the speaker can tell whether they understand the main points of the speech or if he or she needs to go back over something. The audience knows the speaker is interested in them; thus, they pay better attention to him or her than to a speaker who ignores their presence. Eye contact is a simple tool that carries a lot of weight. Looking at people almost *commands* them to look at you and, at the very least, pretend to listen. It supplies you with valuable feedback that is essential to getting your point across to your audience.

One final word is needed about eye contact. There is an old gimmick that speakers are often told to use if they find it difficult to look at their audience. They are told to look over their audience's head to give the illusion of looking at them. Unfortunately, in most cases, this merely gives the appearance of looking over their heads. Unless you are in a large auditorium where your audience is more than ten feet from you, this advice probably won't work. *The best procedure is to maintain frequent eye contact with as much of your audience as possible, thereby keeping their interest and receiving their feedback.*

Posture

Posture is the manner in which you "hold" your body; your pose. Good posture when speaking to an audience is just as important for maintaining the audience's interest and avoiding distractions as it was when you were a child and your mother told you to stand up straight and not to slouch. A comfortable stance is achieved by placing your feet directly below your shoulders and distributing your weight evenly on both feet. By doing this you will avoid many of the unnecessary movements that often accompany nervousness. Shifting weight from foot to foot and swaying from side to side or back and forth can be avoided when you take the proper posture stance. *Movement attracts attention.* We have a tendency to watch what is moving. If you sway, shift weight or tap your foot vigorously, your audience will pay attention to the movement and not to what you are saying. Essentially, poor posture can lead to losing your audience.

Almost all speaking situations require you to use a lectern or podium. Podiums come in all sizes, shapes and styles. You may be using a free-standing model or one that sits on top of a table. Whatever type you use, remember that *the podium is there for you to place your notes on and/or to rest your hands, not to lean on!* Leaning on the podium not only causes poor posture but can be dangerous or embarrassing. Depending on how sturdy the podium is, it could fall, taking you with it. This could cause injury to the body or at the very least the ego. We've discussed the main fear of public speaking—fear of looking foolish. Just imagine how you would feel sprawled out on the floor, your notes scattered around and all eyes on you. So, do yourself a favor; don't lean on the podium.

The question of whether you must remain behind the podium during the majority of your speech often arises. The answer to this is "no." However, there should be a reason for any movement away from the podium: to add emphasis to a point, or to be closer to the audience for some appeal. This does not mean pacing from side to side or wandering through your audience. This type of movement will distract from your presentation. *The best rule to follow is that if there is no concrete reason to move, don't.* Moving toward your audience implies informality, and since most speaking situations are formal occasions, it is usually best to remain behind the podium. You must also remember that any notes you are using will remain at the podium. If you need to refer to them and you are away from them, it could cause an unnecessary break in your delivery.

By following these simple rules, you will avoid unnecessary movement that distracts from what you are saying. Remember, there is room for movement—no one wants to watch a statue for any length of time—but it must be appropriate.

Gestures

Gestures are an appropriate way to add movement to your speech. Gesturing is the use of your hands to add emphasis to important points in your speech. It is one of the least-used tactics of beginning speakers.

You have probably heard people say, "If I tied your hands behind your back, you couldn't say anything." This, of course, refers to the fact that most of us use our hands a great deal to gesture when we are talking to others; all too often when we deliver a speech, we fail to use this most important device. Speakers grip the podium until they achieve "white-knuckle syndrome," clasp their hands behind their back, thrust their hands into their pockets, cross their arms tightly across their chest or let their arms hang limp at their

Well-placed gestures add interest to your speech.

sides. In doing these things, they ignore an everyday habit of using gestures to talk with, and they lose one of the best attention-getters available to the speaker. As we have said before, movement attracts attention, and well-placed gestures add interest to what you are saying. You have literally hundreds of gestures available to you, so practice using them during the content of your speech. This doesn't mean that you must gesture for every idea. Over-gesturing and repetitive gestures can be distracting. However, the use of your hands and arms to accentuate important points will certainly add to your delivery. So try to relax and do what comes naturally. Let your hands help you speak.

Tell Them Where You Live Exercise

Purpose: The purpose of this exercise is to show the speaker how important and natural the use of gestures is.

Procedure:

1. Stand behind the podium.
2. Clasp your hands behind your back.
3. Using *no* hand gestures or signals, give directions from the room you are in to your home's front door.

Facial Expressions

Your face can be an invaluable aid in making your speech interesting. Your **facial expressions**, or animation of your facial features, allow you to convey what you are feeling. In informal situations we often let our facial expressions tell the story just as much as our verbal message. However, when we approach the podium to present our speeches, very often we wear a stoic, expressionless mask. We do this subconsciously to hide our nervousness or fear. But in allowing this to occur, we severely limit our ability to tell our story. People watch other people's faces. If you show your audience that you are interested and sincere by your facial expressions, they will more readily join in the message you are sending. By relaxing and allowing your face to show what you are feeling, you can greatly enhance the quality of your performance. If what you are saying is amusing, smile; if you're trying to impress your audience with the importance of a statement, let your face show it. Again, facial expressions are natural. By allowing your face to show your audience your intent, you will not only get your message across with more clarity and interest, but feel more relaxed and sincere.

Appearance

Your **appearance**, the clothes you wear and the way you are groomed, will have an effect on how your speech is accepted by your audience. Since your audience will be looking at you, it is important to present the best image you can. First impressions are often lasting impressions. At the very least, they start your audience's opinions about your authority and credibility working. Some people may tune you out before you say your first word depending on how you look. Others will listen more intently because you look like someone they can respect.

In the classroom situation, appearance may not affect your audience as much as it will in a business or public meeting, but it does play a part. Generally speaking, most dress codes have been abolished and students dress as they please. If you wear jeans and T-shirts to class normally, it is acceptable attire for the day you are scheduled to speak. As a matter of fact, turning up dressed in a suit when you usually wear jeans might distract your audience from your speech. They may wonder why you've dressed differently and if it isn't apparent when you start your speech, they may think about your attire rather than listen to what you are saying.

Sometimes you may want to dress differently to make a point or use clothing as a gimmick in your speech. For example: a student was doing a speech on donating blood and he dressed as Count Dracula. It served its purpose well. The audience was immediately curious about his costume and it related directly to his topic. Dressing differently can be effective if it is done for a specific reason.

It is wise to do a little homework when you are asked to present a speech outside of the class. Find out how people usually dress for the occasion and adapt your apparel to their mode unless there is a reason not to do so. Dressing as your audience does will often help tie you to them, making them more receptive and you more comfortable.

However you dress for the occasion remember that a neat, clean appearance will always start you out on the right foot.

Now, let's talk about hairstyles. Remember your eyes are one of the most important avenues of communication. Make sure your audience can see them. Any hairstyle which obscures your vision will act as a barrier and, hence, cut you off from your audience. Likewise, caps and sunglasses are a hindrance unless they are used as a visual aid for your speech.

Remember, your appearance sets the mood of your speech before you even begin to speak. Your attire and grooming are vital components of your delivery.

By combining these nonverbal skills with effective verbal skills, you will be assured of an effective presentation.

Visual Presentations

Another element of delivery that must be examined when preparing your delivery is the use of audio/visual aids. **Audio/visual aids** are such devices as posters, pictures, charts and recordings that are used by the speaker to aid in getting his or her speech across to the audience.

Posters, pictures and charts are valuable aids in explaining and clarifying elements of your message. When using one of these devices, you must make sure it follows a few simple rules:

1. *The visual aid must be large enough for your audience to see.* This means that vacation snap shots and most photographs from books or magazines must be enlarged to be seen by the majority of your audience. The opaque projector is a useful machine for this purpose. You will probably need to schedule it in advance with either the A.V. department of your school or your instructor. You will also need to know how to use the machine. Avoid complications by practicing with it. Slide projectors are also useful if your photo is available in this medium. Charts can be used on the opaque projector or transferred to a transparency and used on a machine called the overhead projector. Computer-generated graphics are also a source for visual aids which can be transferred to trans-parencies for easier use at the podium. The same arrangements will probably need to be made for the availability and use of this machine as with the opaque projector. Many times the most effective and easiest way of presenting your visual aid

Visual aids can help to give you confidence at the podium.

is to make a poster of it. Posters should be large enough to be seen, neatly lettered or drawn, and easy to handle.

2. *The visual aid should be controllable.* Since the purpose of a visual aid is to help you and not hinder your performance, you must be able to control and handle this device. This means that you should know how to operate any machine you use. Fumbling with switches, focusing, etc., will only detract from your purpose. Positioning the aid is also important. If you are using a poster, you must have a place to secure it so it does not fall down or bend over. It should also allow your hands to be free to point out issues or gesture. If you must turn your back to the audience to refer to a chart, you will be breaking eye contact, which will detract from your presentation. Remember you are talking to your audience, not to your visual aid. Another point to remember is that passing items or pictures around to your audience during your speech will draw their attention away from you. If you must pass something out to your audience, do so after your speech or have enough copies so that everyone has a copy and can refer to it only when you ask them to do so.

3. *The visual aid must be pertinent to your topic.* Since the purpose of a visual device is to add understanding or interest to your words, the item should be specifically related to what you are talking about. Visual aids are important, but including something just to draw attention that isn't important to your purpose is distracting. Showing a picture of a lion when your speech is on tigers and you couldn't find a suitable picture of a tiger is unnecessary and distracting. Charts on statistics are useful, but presenting unimportant statistics just to use a visual aid is confusing.

When used properly, visual aids are excellent devices for speakers. By following these suggestions, you can assure yourself that your presentation will be aided greatly.

Audio Presentations

The use of records, tapes and CDs can add to your presentation of a musical subject. The use of a tape player is fine for one selection, but if you are planning to skip around through a recording, you may wish to investigate portable CD players because the cuing of the selection is so much simpler and more accurate, and the sound reproduction so much superior to tapes. Whatever device you use for the presentation of your sound, keep these rules in mind when preparing for audio examples:

1. *The audio presentation should be pertinent to your topic.* Just as a visual aid must refer to your topic, an audio device must add to your information on the topic. Playing a selection from a rock album is inappropriate when your topic is jazz development.

2. *The audio presentation must be clear and easy to hear.* This requirement means that the volume must be such that it can be heard by all the audience without blasting the eardrums of the closest audience member. The recording must also be of good quality to be understood by the audience. Static, poor tape quality or scratched records will detract from, rather than aid, your presentation.

3. *The audio presentation must be controllable.* You must know how to use the machine responsible for the production of the sound, as well as how and when to start and stop the machine. If you are using several selections, be sure they are easily cued (ready to be started quickly) without searching for them.

Audio presentations can provide excellent examples for topics not available in any other form. Just be sure they help you rather than detract from your presentation.

The most important thing to remember about audio/visual devices is that they are an aid to you in developing your topic. This means that you should fill the primary time limit with your speech and not let the device do your presentation for you. You must be in control at all times. Use audio/visual aids, they are valuable tools for clarification and audience understanding; all too often, they are overlooked by the novice speaker. Just remember not to let them detract from the speaker—you.

Use of Special Equipment and People as Props

Occasionally, you may wish to use a movie clip (*just* a clip) to illustrate a point. Cue the video properly and make sure you have made arrangements to have the equipment in the speaking room for the presentation.

Often a demonstration may include a person who has agreed to help serve as "guinea pig" for your presentation. Make sure you introduce the person to the audience, provide him or her with seating until he or she is needed and generally be courteous when dealing with this helper. You tell your audience a lot about yourself as you relate to this person.

With all the technical details attended to, you are now ready to practice the speech, to insure that all the elements we have discussed in this chapter focus on the presentation.

Practicing the Delivery

The final element of a well-delivered speech depends upon one essential aspect of preparation—practice. No speech can be delivered to the best of the speaker's ability without practice. You must take the time to deliver your speech aloud several times before actual presentation to your audience. This does not mean memorizing the contents, but it does mean rehearsing with your notes until you know the essence of the speech. There is no way to adequately time a presentation or to work on the verbal and nonverbal aspects of speaking without practice. Get a family member or a friend to listen to you, or record your speech on tape and listen to it. If you own a camcorder use it to hear and see your rehearsal. At the very least, practice it aloud when you are by yourself. Try rehearsing it in front of a full-length mirror to see what you are doing as well as hear what you are saying. We may become self-conscious in practicing this way, but it is the final key to presenting a polished performance. Nothing is as effective as practicing your speech as much as possible before its actual delivery. There is no substitute for practice. Practice allows you to time your speech, hear your voice, and improve on your nonverbal delivery. It cuts down on fear and apprehension and improves on your ultimate goal—presenting a speech that your audience will listen to and learn from. *Practice.*

Let's summarize the important aspects of delivery:

1. Establish eye contact with your audience.
2. Use good posture and avoid unnecessary movement.
3. Use gestures to add interest and emphasis to your speech.
4. Use facial expressions to animate and enforce your comments.
5. Dress appropriately and be well groomed.
6. Choose your language carefully and be sure your audience understands the words you use.
7. Use proper grammar.
8. Pronounce your words correctly.
9. Enunciate the words you use in a clear voice.
10. Use rate, volume and pitch to establish mood in your speech.

11. Be creative in using transitions from point to point.
12. Use the rules for handling audio/visual aids to clarify ideas in presenting your speech.
13. Practice your speech aloud.

Notes You Take to the Podium

One of the best "security blankets" that a speaker can have as he or she takes the podium is a sound collection of notes to help in the delivery. These notes should be written on only one side of 6x8 index cards rather than a sheet of notebook paper. (Paper rattles.) The cards should contain only the basic points of the outline of the speech: a date or two, a fact or number which you found difficult to memorize—any short phrase which will trigger your mind to produce the supportive material you have selected in your preparation. These three suggestions may help you in devising just what your notes should include:

1. *Make them simple.* Do not put whole paragraphs on your note cards. You may be tempted to read them. Just a word per major point should be sufficient to recall the whole thought to your mind.

2. *Have them ordered and numbered.* Nothing is quite so frustrating to an audience (or so embarrassing to a speaker) as watching a speaker fumble over a stack of note cards trying to find the right one. Ideally, one or two cards should suffice for a three- to five-minute speech. However, should you need more, carefully number them and check the order after you place them on the podium. One of my students claimed that some unseen hand had secretly shuffled his note cards when he wasn't looking. Don't let this happen to you.

3. *Make them brief.* Like the suggestion above to make them simple, this suggestion deals with the style of delivery. One glance is all you have time for between points. All the rest of the time you should be maintaining eye contact with your audience. In that glance you should be able to orient yourself to the note card and find the next point you wish to cover. Leave plenty of space between points. White paper (space) helps your eye select the next word. Say you are giving three hints on cleaning your car. You have covered removal of tar and you have told us to wash the inside of the windows. Your last point is dusting the dashboard and arm rests and applying a shining oil to keep the surfaces clean. You glance down at

the note card and see "3.) Dust and apply shine. Ex: ice cream cone." This is all you need to remember the last point and your example about the time your nephew upended his chocolate ice cream cone on the dashboard. Here is what your note card might look like for that speech:

   I. Tar.
      A. Gasoline.
      B. Elbow grease.
  II. Polish windows inside.
      A. Smoke residue.
      B. Smudges.
 III. Dust and apply shine.
     Ex: Ice cream cone.

Your introduction and conclusion are firmly in mind so those points probably need not appear on the notes. With the information shown you could easily tell an audience in three-to-five minutes how to clean their cars.

Conclusion

You have now seen how the culminating activity of practicing your speech can insure a more fluent, effective delivery. Bearing in mind the **nonverbal** elements of delivery (eye contact, posture, gesture and facial expression) along with the **verbal** elements (grammar, language choice, proper pronunciation), you have seen how you can prepare yourself for the actual performance of the speech before a live audience. Again, we suggest that you *relax!* You have done all you can beforehand. Remember, your perception of the world is like no other individual's. You alone can open the treasure of your perception through the magical, stimulating avenue of public speaking.

Study Questions

1. Describe how sound is produced.
2. Discuss how rate, volume and pitch combine to create the tone of your speech.
3. Why are vocal dynamics important to the speaker and audience?
4. Outline any vocal problems you have and a plan for correcting them.
5. Tell how nonverbal elements help you "sell" your speech.
6. Why is word choice important in delivery?
7. Choose a topic and list different audio/visual aids you could use for that speech.
8. Why should you practice your speech before actually delivering it?

Key Words

Appearance	Nonverbal
Audio/Visual aids	Pitch
Content	Posture
Delivery	Pronunciation
Diaphragm	Rate
Enunciation	Register
Eye contact	Semantics
Facial Expressions	Tone
Gestures	Transition
Grammar	Verbal
Larynx	Volume

6

Types of Speeches and Speakers

Chapter Six Outline

I. The Informative speech covers the majority of speeches you hear or give.
   A. The main purpose is to dispense knowledge.
      1. To achieve this goal, it is important for the speaker to know exactly what he or she wants the audience to know.
      2. To achieve this goal, it is important for the speaker to keep the audience's interest.
         a. Provide material unknown to the audience.
         b. Approach the subject in a novel or unique way.
   B. There are five main types of informative speeches.
      1. The descriptive speech is used to share very vivid, specific pictures about the topic.
      2. The demonstration speech shows how an object is made or how it works.
      3. The definition speech explains an idea to the audience.
      4. Lectures are usually used for structured educational purposes.
      5. Reports are usually used in business settings with a limited, designated topic.

II. There is a fundamental difference between informative and persuasive speaking.
   A. A speech to inform encourages gaining new knowledge.
   B. A speech to persuade influences the audience.

III. The purpose of a persuasive speech is to alter the listener's thoughts or behavior.
   A. There are three general types of persuasive speeches.
      1. A speech to stimulate increases beliefs already held by your audience.
      2. The speech to convince converts the listener's thoughts to agree with those of the speaker.
      3. A speech to activate motivates the audience to action.
   B. To persuade you must address the needs present in your audience.
      1. Physical needs are easy to tap into.
      2. Philosophical needs are often difficult to identify.
      3. The more needs addressed, the larger the audience support for your solution.
      4. Use a combination of emotional and functional appeals to "sell" your topic.
   C. In order to develop and defend your belief, you must know what kind of claim you are making in your argument.

1. A claim is a proposition.
2. There are three types of propositions.
   a. A proposition of fact argues whether something is true or not.
   b. A proposition of value argues right or wrong.
   c. A proposition of policy proposes action be taken.

   D. Persuasive speeches must be logical and carefully reasoned.

   E. Any speaker's persuasion is subject to ethical scrutiny.

VI. One method of organizing persuasive speeches is known as motivated sequence.
   A. The first step is getting your audience's attention.
   B. The second step is the need step, which provides the audience with the problem.
   C. The third step is one of satisfaction which provides a solution to the problem.
   D. The fourth step is visualization, which shows the audience the improvement your plan provides.
   E. The final step is one of action: Calling the audience to a specific action.

V. It is important to test your evidence.
   A. Ask yourself "Is the evidence recent?"
   B. Determine if your source is unbiased.
   C. Ask "Is the material relevant?"

VI. The purpose of special occasion speaking (entertaining speeches) is simply to keep the audience's attention and interest.
   A. It need not necessarily be humorous.
   B. There are several types of special occasion speaking.
   Types:
          Introduction
          Welcome
          Keynote
          Tributes
          The Stand-up Comic
          The Traveler
          The Hobby Buff
          Presentation
          Nominating
          Acceptance
          Commencement
          Farewell

Chapter Six

Types of Speeches and Speakers

Introduction

"Your assignment for Tuesday is to give an informative speech." Very often students in speech classes are told to give a specific type of speech. These distinctions may be more imagined than real. In separating types of speeches we are faced with the fact that the three main types (informative, persuasive and entertaining) are often combined in one speech. Any speaker worth his salt will keep his audience awake during his presentation—in a way *entertaining* them. Further, he will provide information previously unknown by his audience, thus *informing* them. Frequently the information provided in a speech will motivate the audience in some manner, thus *persuading*. However, to clarify our discussion we will take each type of speech, explain its distinctive qualities, and provide examples.

Informative Speeches

One of the most common speeches is a speech to inform. **Informative speeches** are presented with the intent of increasing the audience's knowledge about a subject. A well-focused, organized and effectively delivered speech of this type will increase the audience's understanding on a particular topic. For a speech to be an effective tool of information it must focus on *exactly* the material or idea the speaker wishes his or her audience to learn from the speech. The purpose, then, is in some way to offer the audience information they do not already possess. This can be accomplished in one of two ways: (1) by providing material unknown to the audience, or (2) by approaching the subject in a novel or unique manner. While the general purpose remains the same for all informative speaking situations, the direction and style in which the data are presented can fall into several different categories: descriptive, demonstration, definition, reports and lectures. Understanding these groups will help you decide the best approach to use for your topic and audience.

Descriptive Speeches

A **descriptive speech** is used when the speaker wants his or her audience to share a very vivid specific picture about the topic. In a descriptive speech your purpose is to create a picture the audience can clearly visualize. Description is effective only when the language chosen is very specific and graphically detailed. Notice the difference between the following descriptions:

A wall divided the property.

and

An irregular grey stone fence,
neglected and overgrown,
separated the property.

Using sensory examples that relate to size, color, shape, etc., paint a much more effective mental image. Use the descriptive form for your informational speech if you wish to have your audience feel and see the person, place, object or event they are learning.

Examples of descriptive speeches could include: informing the audience about the effects of lead poisoning on children, describing Beatlemania to a 16-year-old, providing an impression of what it is like to be visually handicapped to a sighted audience and creating excitement as you describe your first sight of the Magic Kingdom.

Demonstration Speeches

The **demonstration speech** shows how something is done or made, how something works or how something happens. Its goal is to present a process that the audience can follow in clear, comprehensive order. The most effective demonstration speeches use numerous visual aids to show a step-by-step explanation of the "how to" or employ an actual live demonstration with verbal instructions. Actual demonstration should be employed when the entire process being covered can occur within the time limit of the speech. When the process would take a longer time than allotted, visual aids, such as a craft project in different states of completion, can help bridge the accelerated time sequence. Due to the purpose of this type of informative speech, it will most likely be organized in chronological order requiring you to lead your audience from point to point with carefully worded transitions.

The two mistakes most often made during a demonstration speech are (1) failing to cover the physical demonstration with verbal explanations and (2) talking to your visual aid rather than your audience. *Tell your audience what you are doing; let them see your face and your poster.* In addition, pay attention as you set up your speech so that you have everything you need for the demo and have things arranged in an easy-to-use order.

Examples of speeches that work well as demonstrations include: hanging wall paper, programming a VCR, cording wool, making a paper airplane and stir-frying Chinese vegetables.

Definition Speeches

A **definition speech** explains some concept, idea or more concrete subject to the audience. Since informative speeches of all types deal with information the audience does not know, the speech to define explains a term, object or new idea. This type of speech is most effective when audience analysis indicates that the information is new for the majority of the listeners. While some audiences will sit still for a review or "rehash" of yesterday's news, most will not. This does not preclude doing a speech on a subject that a significant percentage of the audience knows, just approach it in a unique way. This form of speech can be used to define creative, thoughtful topics as well as complex subjects.

Examples of descriptive speeches are those that might explain the meaning of karma or how child abuse can be emotional, not only physical. They can also answer such questions as "What is HIV?" "What defines an impressionist painting?" or "What is the 'year of the woman'?"

Lectures

Lectures are informative speeches given by experts, usually for educational purposes. You may just be getting used to the college lecture class. Instruction is often conducted for a class of 40 to 150 students with the instructor talking for the majority of the class period. As you move from class to class, be aware of the various techniques your instructors use to capture and keep your attention during the lecture. Some speakers will use elaborate diagrams on the blackboard or employ transparencies and an overhead projector. Others will use models as they describe a certain chemical reaction or an intricate computer system. All these examples are attempts to disseminate information. They clarify discussion of a given discipline from mathematics to physics, from English composition to theater art. Often humor is employed to "punch" a point home. Sometimes a question is thrown out by the speaker to encourage discussion or check to see if the message sent is the message received. This type of speech need not be dull. You will be able to witness the skill with which your best instructors move the class from idea to idea, questioning, enlightening, involving the class in the learning process. Be aware. Many of these same techniques can be employed by you in your informative speeches.

Reports

A **report** is a type of speech, usually used in a business setting, with a limited designated topic. These presentations explain the results of some data, survey, committee project or market analysis. They are technical and require attention to detail and accuracy, but need not be boring. Flip-charts, transparencies, and other aids in the form of charts and helpful graphics are frequently used to further illustrate important points.

A word of caution seems appropriate before moving on to the next type of speech. Remember that you are only providing data to your audience, you are not trying to influence them or motivate them to accomplish something. The ultimate outcome of your speech may very well be that the audience (or at least some members of the audience) will be moved to take some action. However, this is not the intent of the informative speech and should not be implied in the manner in which you present your speech. For example, you present a speech on the special effects in a particular movie; your intent is to explain how the technicians accomplished these particular effects. At the conclusion of your speech some audience members may decide to go see the film you have been discussing. This is an outcome of your speech, but not your purpose. Motivation is the purpose of the next type of speech we will discuss.

Informative vs. Persuasive Speaking

Students are frequently required to present both informative and persuasive speeches. Although the distinction between these sometimes blurs, there is a fundamental difference between the two styles. An informative speech encourages gaining new knowledge and understanding. A **persuasive speech** tries to influence the thoughts, feelings or activities of the listener. Specifically, an informative speech *provides data* on an issue, while a persuasive speech *seeks to influence* the audience's beliefs or actions.

Notice the difference in the intent of the following two specific purposes, even though they are both on the same general topic. The first is a speech to inform, the second to persuade.

> The audience will understand the conditions
> necessary to cure tobacco.

> The audience will not chew or smoke tobacco.

While informative and persuasive speeches share many elements of sending a clear, effective message, they are separated by distinctly different goals. Becoming an effective speaker has been covered in the other chapters of this text, but effective *persuasive* speaking requires some special attention.

Persuasive Speaking

One of the most rewarding and time-honored speeches is the speech to persuade. Unlike the speech to inform, the persuasive speech uses data and emotional appeal to go beyond the realm of education into directing how that knowledge should be thought of or used. Understand at the outset that the audience will resist change. Humankind is definitely subject to the principle of physics called inertia which says a body at rest tends to remain at rest. We feel secure in patterns of behavior already established, concepts already accepted, beliefs already held. The longer we have held certain beliefs or have engaged in certain patterns of behavior, the harder it is to break those patterns and try something different.

While the general goal of all persuasive arguments will remain the same, to change something, the exact intent will differ on what kind and extent of change you wish to make.

Speeches To Stimulate

This type of speech is the easiest of the persuasive types to reach its goal because the intended audience is already leaning in the direction you want them to be. In a **speech to stimulate**, your purpose is simply to increase and strengthen those attitudes and beliefs already held by your audience. Change is still required, but only the *degree* of the involvement needs to be intensified.

A coach's speech about winning to his team before a game, a twelve-step program member's "experience, strength and hope" and the minister preaching to his congregation are all speeches designed to stimulate.

Breaking the inertia can at times be difficult, but it is certainly easier than convincing them to believe it in the first place.

Speeches To Convince

The **speech to convince** is used when the speaker needs or desires to convert his or her listeners' decisions and thoughts about someone or something to the speaker's point of view.

Requesting that your parents eliminate your curfew now that you're in college, addressing a jury and convincing overtaxed citizens that schools are worthy investments for our future are all examples of speeches to convince. It is important to note at this point that while a speech of this type implies action that may be necessary at some future time, you are only trying to achieve a *mental shift* by the conclusion of the speech.

Speeches To Activate

Speeches to activate are used to motivate the audience to action. This is the only style of persuasive speech that totally overcomes all the inertia residing within your listeners. The ultimate purpose of this speech is to move your audience to do something. This is the speech that can change behavior. The persuasive speaker offers the audience a new way of looking at things, challenges accepted modes of behavior and offers an alternative to the status quo. In Meredith Wilson's *Music Man*, when Harold Hill is trying to sell his boys' band to the town of River City, he must first provide a need for the change. He attacks the only existing source of recreation in the small Iowa town—the pool hall. He suggests that there is "Trouble right here in River City . . . with a capital 'T' and that rhymes with 'P' and that stands for Pool!" Having demolished the existing recreational source, he provides an alternative in the form of a boys' band and wins over support for his cause: he persuades his audience.

Persuasion then, is the process of moving your audience from the point where all are thinking in different directions to the point where all minds are focused upon your arguments and are accepting your solution to the problem.

Types of Needs

In the initial stages of your persuasion you must address yourself to the needs present in your audience. Consider for a moment the kinds of needs you have as an individual in society. **Physical needs** like food, clothing and shelter come immediately to mind. Any speaker who suggests a program of buying groceries more economically, lowering fuel bills or providing a more efficient smoke detector will probably gain immediate audience attention because he or she is speaking about a need all members of the audience share.

Philosophical needs may be difficult to identify. Friends and loved ones are important to most people. Hints about how to improve interpersonal relationships would probably be welcomed by any audience. We all share a need to feel we are contributing to our society in some measurable way. We have goals and dreams. The complex personality of each member of the audience may seem to present a challenge too large in scope to any speaker, but if the presenter keeps the needs clearly before him, he can galvanize his audience into a single unit and move them toward his solution of the need he addresses.

In addition to the two areas just mentioned, we should consider the area of needs which combines these two. Love, sex and self-esteem are all areas in our lives which cannot be dealt with by the individual alone. To satisfy the needs in these corners of our lives we must depend upon contact with our fellow-creatures. Presenting on these needs may take a little longer, but they are very significant to the audience.

The speaker wants to gain the largest support he can from his audience. To do this he may have to address more than one need. Care must be taken not to confuse the audience, but a good rule of thumb is "the more needs addressed, the larger the audience support for your solution."

As you look for ways to address these basic human needs, you will be faced with a number of decisions as to what seems to be the best persuasive approach. Should you concentrate on **emotional appeals** (those appeals that pull at our hearts) or **functional** (factual) **appeals** (those appeals that work on our heads)? The answer to this dilemma is use both. Combine the functional appeals with the emotional ones and you will have a sales pitch that covers all the bases. Studies show that emotional appeals are very effective persuasive tools in the short term and that functional appeals have more lasting results. Therefore, a persuasive speech that grabs the audience by their emotions and then gives them facts to back them up will optimize the results generated by each. Let's say that you wish to persuade your audience that they can do something about the homeless in America. Your specific purpose is this: At the conclusion of your speech each member of the audience will sign a petition demanding your state legislature allocate money for the building of new overnight shelters. If you use emotional appeals, show pictures of homeless people that include women and children, talk about people freezing to death in cardboard boxes, relate the diet of someone on the streets, etc.; then follow up with statistics estimating the number of displaced persons compared to the number of beds available in existing shelters—factual appeals. You will have your audience asking if they can help circulate petitions, not merely sign one. Emotions stirred, followed and integrated with cold, hard facts are mighty persuasive tools.

 ## Propositions

As you prepare to develop and defend your belief in a persuasive speech you must know what kind of claim you are making in your argument. Are you arguing that some objective belief is or isn't true but not saying it is right or wrong? Then your proposition is one of *fact*. If you are arguing that something is right or wrong, works or doesn't work, then your proposition is one of *value*. When you propose that some action be taken, your proposal is one of *policy*. Examples:

proposition of fact	Lee Harvey Oswald was the lone assassin of John F. Kennedy.
proposition of value	Plea bargaining is undermining our legal system
proposition of policy	The electoral college should be abolished in favor of a popular vote election of the president.

No matter what your claim, you will have to persuade your audience to agree with your argument by providing a means of persuasion.

Logic

We all know what is meant by the term **logic**; it implies a carefully reasoned, orderly succession of details leading to an understandable conclusion. We laugh at the comedians and comediennes who break the logical chain; who appear to be "spacey," (i.e., illogical). When lovely Gracie Allen (George Burns' late wife) was told about a friend's death, she replied, "Oh, I hope she didn't die of anything serious." Alice, in her incredible journey through Wonderland, is constantly being reminded that the fantastic world she has entered is not bound by the rules of logic with which she is familiar.

A tour through illogical and unsupported evidence is a sure-fire way to lose your audience and your argument. Be sure to document your contentions. Statistics, narratives, anecdotes and analogy are effective ways of championing your cause. Testimony, sensory evidence and comparing/contrasting are all logical ways of selling your proposition.

One way of depicting logic is to present some examples of what is illogical. For this reason, we offer you ten fallacies to logical thinking. Make certain your persuasive arguments avoid these, and you are probably being logical in your persuasion.

Note: The examples given are *fallacies*, types of arguments *to be avoided*.

1. *Dicto Simpliciter*: Unqualified generalization. "Sugar is a source of energy; therefore, the more sugar I eat, the more energy I have."

2. *Hasty Generalization*: Too few instances to support the conclusion. "You can't sell your car; I can't sell my car; my friend, George, can't sell his car. I conclude that no private owners are able to sell their own cars."

3. *Post Hoc*: Cause-effect relationship unclear. "Let's not take Joe with us; every time we take him we get a flat tire."

4. *Contradictory Premise*: Premise #1 contradicts premise #2. (#1) "If God can do anything, (#2) can He make a stone so heavy He cannot lift it?"

5. *Ad Misericordiam*: Ignoring the argument and appealing to sympathy. "I've just come from a bad siege in the hospital so you should believe me."

6. *False Analogy*: A comparison of two very different things. "My wife treats my arguments like a meat grinder."

7. *Hypothesis Contrary to Fact*: That statement which assumes something that is not fact. "If George Bush had won his second election to the presidency, the American public would not have such a high unemployment rate."

8. *Poisoning the Well*: Slander or personal attack on an opponent in an argument. "My opponent is a liar. You'll never be able to believe anything he says."
9. *Loaded Question*: "Are you still cheating on your taxes?"
10. *Either/or Question*: Two extreme choices, one good, one evil. "We can continue this administration's deficit-producing policies that bankrupt America and her people, or we can elect a new, honest, non-corrupt government by electing Candidate XYZ."

To persuade your audience, present your objections to the status quo and formulate a plan to meet those objectives. Bear in mind that an audience must be carefully and logically led to your point of view with clear and honest evidence.

Ethics

Without getting preachy, we must say a few words about the **ethics** involved in persuasion. We live in an "oral culture." We spend a large amount of time listening. We receive most of our world news auditorily. News reporting is pre-analyzed, pre-cut, pre-thought; all we have to do is absorb it. Because our media coverage is freer than any in the world, we probably receive factual, accurate coverage of people and events. But, because of the lack of sufficient time to present all the data which supports a given conclusion, we, the audience, have to depend upon the integrity of the reporter giving the story, whether it is coverage of a war in Bosnia or coverage of a local fire. We, the television-viewing public, assume the anchorperson is honest, that he or she is telling the truth.

The same is true of your audience for your persuasion speech. They assume you are telling the truth. Your obligation as a speaker is to be honest with your audience, seeking the most recent factual support for your arguments and maintaining strict discipline and accuracy in reporting your sources. The fact that we are all not experts on the United States' fiscal policy does not mean we cannot talk about it or hold an opinion about that policy. What we speakers do need to remember is that an audience is likely to want more than our word for it when we are discussing such fiscal policy. We will need authorities in the field to support our contention: facts, opinion, and evidence—all marshalled to support our line of reasoning. This means that you will probably have to include more quotes and documentation in your persuasive speech than is necessary in an informative speech.

Another question that arises concerning ethics is, "Since there

No matter what our own opinions are, we as speakers have an obligation to our audience to be honest in presenting our arguments.

are obviously more ways of looking at my topic than the one I am proposing, should I mention those opposing viewpoints?'' The answer to this is ''maybe.'' If you believe that your audience is either unaware, apathetic or already leaning in your direction, then don't fuel fires that don't exist. You are not morally or ethically responsible for destroying your own goal, which is what could occur if you bring up arguments against your point of view. On the other hand, if you believe that these counter views are widespread and probably well known by your audience or they are leaning towards one or more of these other ways of looking at your topic, then it becomes necessary for you to comment on them. If your audience falls into the latter category, then you will probably want to build a section into your speech that will show why your view is better and more logical than the opposition. This will take part of your valuable time, but may be necessary to accomplish your goal.

Be honest, sincere and straightforward with your audience and you will likely be rewarded with their support. Lie to them or attempt to deceive them, even slightly, and they are likely to erupt into an unruly mob bent on "nailing" you. Honesty and integrity include the process of setting up your logic. Avoid the ten fallacies mentioned earlier and your audience will generally feel you are being honest with them.

Organizing a Persuasive Speech

While organizational patterns were discussed in chapter 3, there is another method of organizing that is particularly useful for persuasive speeches known as **motivated sequence**, first developed in the 1930s by Alan Monroe (a speech professor at Purdue). Originally used for sales, this 5-step pattern is used effectively as the organizational process for actuating speeches.

Motivated Sequence

Attention Step	The introduction of your speech; getting the audience's attention and letting them know what your subject is.
Need Step	Body of the Speech; proving to the audience that there is a problem that requires fixing.
Satisfaction Step	Body of the Speech; solves the now established problem by providing a solution to the problem.
Visualization Step	Body of the Speech; getting your audience to see how much better it will be if they adopt your plan and how bad it will be if they don't.
Action	The conclusion of your speech; calls on the audience to do specifically what the speaker asks them to do.

If this sounds familiar it is exactly what Professor Hill did to sell River City that boys' band and is probably how you were sold the last item you bought. Careful attention to these five steps can make your speech to actuate work as well.

Persuasion is difficult. It takes time to set up your arguments and find the needs in your audience to appeal to. But the rewards can be great. The feeling of exhilaration that comes from sensing a room full of people on your side has few equals. And when you get the audience to vote your way, or donate money, you can witness the full advantage of the time and effort you took to present your arguments to that audience.

Tests of Evidence

We have talked a good deal about "evidence" in this section. **Evidence** is the supporting material which gives your arguments a basis. Evidence is fact and opinion which bolsters your points in argument and persuasion. No matter what side of an issue you pick, you will need to have evidence to support your claims. Three tests may be applied to your evidence to give it credence in your audience's mind: 1) Is it recent? 2) Is the source or person you quote unbiased? and 3) Is it relevant? These questions we'll deal with briefly.

Is it recent? If your facts to support a fiscal policy of the U.S. Congress date from 1965, they are interesting, but not necessarily very relevant today. What is the most recent data you can muster to support your claim that Social Security payments need to be cut? Get the most immediate data. Call a broker. Check the *Wall Street Journal.*

Is your source or person unbiased? Many debate partners I've had maintain there is no such thing as an unbiased source. Almost everyone has an "ax to grind." But, because we live in a "free society" with generally free access to facts, you can assume that the information you gain from a large newspaper or newsmagazine is going to be generally unbiased. A line from the "Meet The Press" television panels of the 1950s comes to mind: "The questions do not necessarily reveal the panel member's point of view; it is merely our way of getting a story for you." With the rise of special interest groups and PACs in Washington it becomes harder and harder to find an unbiased source. But you can present for your audience the qualifications of your source and let them make up their minds about the quality of that source.

Is it relevant? This area has to do with emotional appeals. Check to see if the evidence you have provided is addressing the point of your argument, and is not extraneous. To cite endless facts about child abuse when your proposition has to do with sexual harassment in the workplace is irrelevant. Again, the common-sense approach should rule. Just be aware your audience needs to have some basis on which to place your argument, and these tests of evidence may help those whom you are trying to persuade.

Special Occasion Speaking

We now reach that area of speaking commonly referred to as entertaining, after-dinner or **special occasion speaking**. The major purpose of the speech is to keep the audience's attention and interest for a short period of time, usually from 15 to 45 minutes. Humor may be used, but a speaker need not be a comic to entertain an audience. Speeches dealing with the supernatural, genealogy or scuba diving, while apparently disseminating information, can be entertaining. The approach is lighter and you wouldn't seriously try to really sell or persuade with any intent other than enjoyment. In general though, the special occasion speech is prepared and delivered much the same as the informative or persuasive speech. Some special attention and caution needs to be heeded by the speaker who literally speaks after dinner, however. First, the audience members have just eaten and are likely to behave like bears in hibernation by yawning and stretching, and unless there's good ventilation, they may fall asleep. The way to avoid their inattention is to be energetic and fascinating.

Another problem is that they may be drinking. An audience who has just enjoyed a couple of cocktails and a banquet dinner is likely to be slow in reacting to the speaker's words. Be energetic but don't go too rapidly and lose them on the way.

The following types and combinations of presentation styles will generally fulfill your needs if you are asked to present an entertaining speech.

Introduction/Welcome/Keynote Speeches

We all have been members of organizations which occasionally invite special speakers for given programs. When such a speaker is slated and you are given the opportunity to introduce that speaker to your group, remember that the introduction should act as a bridge between that speaker and the audience. Your purpose is a service. It is not an opportunity for you to shine. You want the attention centered upon the speaker.

Try to interview the speaker beforehand. Get to know him or her. Discover insights into his or her life or career which you may use to acquaint the audience with the speaker. Some questions may help you glean the information which will act as a catalyst to

An expert is always an interesting speaker.

galvanize the bonding of the new speaker to your familiar audience
of members.

1. Why was this speaker chosen to appear before your group?
2. What background or experience marks him or her as an
   "expert"?
3. What unique qualities or talents does he or she possess?
4. What does this speaker share in common with your audience?
5. Is there any specific information the speaker would like the
   audience to know about himself or herself?

Notice that the questions suggested above are only the beginning,
but these questions parallel the requirements we suggested earlier
for the introduction to your own speeches: namely, get the attention
of the audience and, more importantly, "tie the speaker to the
audience." Sample Introduction:

Good evening and welcome to our annual Father and Son
banquet here at St. John's Church. I'm sure you got enough
to eat and we would like to thank the Ladies of the Guild for

their wonderful help in feeding this crew tonight. Let's show them our appreciation with a round of applause.

And now, it is my pleasure to introduce you to a man who really belongs at a Father and Son banquet. For ten years he and his wife have acted as foster parents at our community center and home: the first stop for boys 12 to 16 years old when they are released from juvenile detention. His degree in Sociology and Counseling is from the University of Illinois. He is here tonight to talk to both sons and fathers on the topic, "Lessons in Listening." Gentleman, may I present Mr. Jerry Caswell.

By first getting his audience clapping (for the serving ladies), this speaker has "warmed them up" for the guest. He then concentrates on the introduction. The information given is clear, but not too detailed. The introduction has tied the speaker to the audience and presented the topic.

If a separate speech of welcome is used, it's purpose is to make the audience feel important for attending the function, thereby giving them a reason for listening to the speaker. Keynote addresses are usually given at conferences and conventions and may be lengthier speeches than the initial welcoming address. They usually focus on some specific topic that those present have convened to discuss and learn about, such as political platform speeches, and frequently call for unification of purpose and audience.

Tributes

A second example of special occasion speaking we have chosen is speeches that recognize the contributions or achievements of people—living or dead—such as testimonials/toasts, roasts, dedications and eulogies.

The major purpose of this kind of speech is to celebrate the life or accomplishments of someone. Usually someone who is or was close to the person gives examples of the qualities of that person's character the speaker feels are worth remembering, usually emphasizing those positive aspects that will infuse the audience with a warm, kind, optimistic feeling regarding this individual. This is true for testimonials, dedications and eulogies. A "roast," however, attempts to do just the opposite and makes good-natured fun of the object of the speech, usually by employing humor.

Note that a eulogy is not an obituary as a toast is not a biography. Not all dates and details of a person's life are exposed. Rather, it is a time for quiet and sincere reflection upon the significance of one person's life.

The Stand-up Comic

Nothing is so difficult as to "try to be humorous." Ask any professional comic entertainer or writer. Erma Bombeck, whose delightful column appears in papers coast-to-coast, suggested in a recent interview that she was not a good party guest because turning out her column week by week was hard work and her humor could not "just happen." So, although we all enjoy Jay Leno's monologue, we may be hard pressed to duplicate it in our own speaking.

What makes an audience laugh? In our experience in classes, we find the majority of students react and respond to two elements of comedy: exaggeration and the unexpected. If the example is outrageous, they'll generally respond. If it also is unexpected (out of phase, logically) they'll respond. If while the speaker is presenting his speech he can also gently poke fun at himself, the audience is really with him. Joan Rivers, Tim Allen and Carol Burnett have made careers of laughing at themselves.

Poking fun at others, however, is a little more risky and the speaker must be very careful not to satirize a subject his audience believes is serious. A good rule of thumb is to prepare material you yourself would find amusing and present it in a clear, clever way.

Be yourself. Billy Crystal probably does the best impersonation of Billy Crystal. Don't feel you must ape someone else to reap the rewards of laughter. And be able to take the "lumps" if your jokes fail. If you feel inadequate telling a joke, then forget that kind of speech. Choose another type.

The Traveler and the Hobby Buff

These two kinds of speakers are often related. The traveler is often a photographer; and the surfer or scuba diver must travel to pursue his or her sport. When you, the traveler or the hobby buff, are presenting your respective topics, the major factor you must address is the tie-in to the audience. Why should an audience listen or be interested in your hobby of stamp collecting, fascinating as it may be to you? Why should they really be interested in the trip you took to Paris? You share one thing with your audience, humanity. This basic humanity is curious; it wants to know. Watch a child's inquiring mind work. From the time they learn to say it, one of their favorite words is "why?" We adults still possess that quality, too. And the more you can tell your audience about the world, country or environment in which they live, the more your audience's curiosity will be satisfied. Keep them interested by sharing little-known facts about the Eiffel Tower or the financial records of stamp collecting. They'll be interested alright.

Before we leave these two speeches, let's repeat a suggestion we offered in the fifth chapter on visual aids. Slides and movies are intriguing to an audience, but don't let those slides give the speech. You are still the speaker. Keep control of the attention and only use the visuals to support, not deliver, your speech.

Presentation/Nominating/Acceptance Speeches

These three types of speeches have been grouped together due to the similarities of purpose, occasion and delivery. A speech of presentation is given to honor someone for some accomplishment. A good example would be the Thalberg Award presented annually at the Academy Awards to a member of the academy who through her actions has aided in some cause. A nominating speech is used to place someone before a gathered organization for the purpose of electing them to a particular office. An acceptance speech is given by the person receiving the presentation or nomination.

Acknowledgements should be given, but remember to be exact and fairly brief. The delivery should be poised. Furthermore, if the presentation or acceptance includes some sort of token, like a certificate or plaque, both presenter and accepter should handle it carefully and not fumble or hold it upside down.

Commencement/Farewell Speeches

These types of speeches traditionally are given when the speaker is addressing the audience about some type of ending, such as a retirement or graduation. Even though they are at an ending and may recall past deeds or events, they also call forth an image of the future and a new beginning. These speeches should be brief, despite frequent practice to the contrary, and should convey sincere but concise appreciation through the use of good effective speech delivery.

Conclusion

We have now discussed the three major types of speeches with illustrative examples of these types. By deciding early in the preparation procedure just which type you are shooting for, you will save the speech from becoming a multi-headed serpent which will confuse rather than enlighten and interest your audience.

Study Questions

1. Compare and contrast persuasive and informative speeches.
2. Choose one topic and write a specific purpose for each of the three types of persuasive speeches on that same topic.
3. Choose an informative topic and discuss why it would *best* be presented as a descriptive, demonstration or definition speech.
4. Name two types of "entertaining speeches."
5. Name four of the ten fallacies to logic that should be avoided in persuasive speaking.
6. What are the differences among propositions of fact, value and policy?
7. How can the five-step motivated sequence technique help you "sell" your topic?

Key Words

Definition speeches
Demonstration speeches
Descriptive speeches
Emotional appeals
Ethics
Evidence
Fallacies
Functional appeals
Informative speeches
Lectures
Logic
Motivated sequence

Persuasive speeches
Philosophical needs
Physical needs
Proposition of fact
Proposition of policy
Proposition of value
Reports
Special occasion speaking
Speeches to activate
Speeches to convince
Speeches to stimulate

7

Small Group
Communication

Chapter Seven Outline

I. Everyone belongs to groups.
   A. Some groups are formally organized.
   B. Some groups just occur when people gather together.

II. Small groups gather for decision-making purposes.
   A. The number of people in a small group is usually 3 to 13.
   B. Small groups work best when the members meet in face-to-face interaction.
   C. Small groups meet for varying lengths of time.
   D. Small groups meet to accomplish a particular task or achieve a social function.

III. All groups, whatever their purpose, share five characteristics.
   A. Group decisions are usually more accurate than individual decisions.
   B. Groups are able to recall more information than individuals.
   C. Group members are generally committed to the group's decision.
   D. Working in groups is usually more socially rewarding than working alone.
   E. Working in a group takes more time than working alone.

IV. There are rules that make all groups work.
   A. Group members must cooperate for the common good of the group.
   B. Group members must gather information.
      1. Get the facts before making a decision.
      2. Investigate several sources of information.
      3. Take notes on pertinent information.
   C. Group members must share information.
      1. Present the information in a logical way.
      2. Present the information in an understandable manner.
      3. Use appropriate nonverbals to animate your presentation.
      4. Encourage questions.
      5. Use effective listening skills.

V. Group members have specialized functions or roles.
   A. Leadership will occur in groups.
   B. Other group roles may be observed.
      1. Task roles help reach the group's goals.
      2. Maintenance roles help develop a group cohesiveness.
      3. Personal roles frustrate the group's work.

VI. There are a variety of group experiences.
   A. The round-table discussion provides information on a current topic for a large group.
   B. A debate clarifies positions through organized argumentation.
   C. Problem-solving groups provide information on the background and the solutions to problems.

VII. Parliamentary procedure allows a large group to function.
   A. It is based in history.
   B. The details of the procedure are easy to master.
      1. An agenda is necessary.
      2. An unbiased chairperson is an asset.
      3. Keeping records (minutes) is necessary for reference.
      4. Individual members need to participate.

Chapter Seven

Small Group Communication

Introduction

Throughout this text we have referred to the speaking process as if it revolved around only the speaker—you. We cannot leave this impression. Even though you have been the moving force so far, there are times, many times, in which you must function in a group. In fact, most of the public speaking you will do will involve small groups. You have a group you bowl with. You will be assigned to a work detail at your job. You will join civic and religious groups. All of these activities will mean you must speak as part of a group. This chapter will enable you to meet these obligations and feel comfortable as a functioning unit within a larger context. Part of the Western tradition of public speaking we spoke about at the beginning of this book envisioned you as a member of your society—not acting alone, but as a member of the larger unit: your school, your office, your business, your town. These larger groups work to enhance your life by providing information and social contact which are two of the needs we share as human beings. As a thinking, reasoning member of your society, you should be aware of how these groups function to improve your life and the lives of your family and friends.

Definition

A **small group** is a collection of three to thirteen people who meet together, face-to-face, for a period of time to reach a common purpose or goal.

The size of a small group is important to how well the group will perform. Studies indicate the following four characteristics about group size:

Small groups can meet anywhere.

1. Groups of five appear to function better than any other number of people.
2. Groups who have an odd number of members are more efficient than groups composed of an even number of people.
3. In groups composed of 6 to 13 people the quieter members tend to not share their opinions with the group.
4. Groups larger than 13 in number tend to break into subgroups or cliques.

Keeping these characteristics in mind will help you if you are responsible for setting up groups by helping you anticipate problems that might occur from the size of the group. For example, let's say you are a member of a group that has nine people in it. Because of characteristic number three you would know to make an extra effort to get the shy members of your group to contribute their thoughts and feelings to the group. The fact that these people aren't inclined to share their opinions not only means the group may lose valuable input, but also may cause those people to actually withdraw from the group.

The definition refers to "face-to-face interaction," meaning small groups meet together in one place where they cannot only hear each other, but see each other.

This is important so that group members can respond to each other's nonverbal communication as well as their verbal communication. No matter how much teleconferences are praised on TV commercials for "getting the job done," they are, at best, less effective than face-to-face communication in accomplishing the group's goals.

The period of time a group meets together will vary, depending upon the group's purpose. Some short term committees may be able to have one meeting that lasts an hour and accomplishes their task. Other groups, particularly socially oriented ones, may meet daily, weekly or monthly for years. There is no minimum or maximum time qualification for an effective group. The best rule is probably to play it by ear. If the members of a group are accomplishing their task or purpose—fulfilling the function determined when the group formed—it could continue indefinitely. If, on the other hand, little progress is being made, conflicts are arising, or group members fail to come to a consensus, it might be best to disband the group and start anew.

Types of Groups

Reaching a common goal or purpose is why groups form in the first place. Some groups come together to accomplish or achieve a particular task, while others meet as a social function. Groups can also serve both purposes at social events where certain tasks are performed.

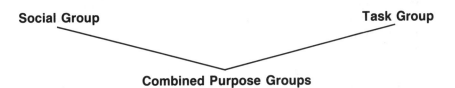

Social Group   **Task Group**

Combined Purpose Groups

An example of a combined purpose group would be five to seven people taking a watercolor class. The purpose for gathering is to learn how to paint with watercolors, making them initially a task-oriented group. However, after the first meeting it becomes obvious that while they wish to learn the watercolor media, the group members also want something to do on the night their class meets. They also are interested in meeting new people. They begin to go out after class for coffee and carry the general socialization back to the class environment.

Some socialization will occur in even the most structured task groups and certain tasks can be accomplished in groups that are primarily social. These aspects of group work are due to the roles individuals assume in group interaction and will be discussed later in our study of small groups. At the present, it is sufficient to be aware that while groups' purposes may be primarily task-oriented or socially oriented, pure groups rarely, if ever, exist. All groups, whatever their purpose, share the same characteristics.

Group Characteristics

1. Group decisions are usually more accurate or correct than individual decisions.
2. Groups usually are able to recall more information than individuals.
3. Being a member of a group generally increases your commitment to the decision made by the group.
4. Working with others in a group is usually more socially rewarding than working alone.
5. Working in a group usually takes more time to complete a task or reach a decision than working as an individual.

Let's look at each of these characteristics in more depth. Group decisions are usually more accurate or correct than individual decisions. This statement means that the conclusions reached by a group will, in most cases, be better or more correct than decisions made on an individual basis. You have probably heard the saying, "two heads are better than one"; that's exactly what this means. When people form a group and contribute opinions and ideas, they can collectively research an issue and come to a judgment more effectively than one person can.

Another factor in reaching a decision is the information collected. This is referred to in the second characteristic listed above. Five people can obviously remember or store five times the amount of knowledge one person can. In addition to increased information, members of the group may trigger or cue the remembrance of some idea in another member's mind, thus leading to more information being shared.

Being a member of a group generally increases your commitment to the decision made by the group. Because of the public nature of working in groups (i.e., sharing personal opinions with other people rather than merely thinking about them) we tend to be more dedicated to the outcome of the group process. Voicing and hearing our thoughts and feelings shared with other people tends to make us more compatible with the group's members. Because groups give us a chance to make our views known, we increase our participation with the group. This participation in the decision making increases our dedication to the decision made by the group, even if it isn't our personal choice.

Man is primarily a social animal. In other words, people receive their greatest benefits from interaction with other people. That is why working with others in a group is usually more socially rewarding than working alone. Of course, there are difficulties that exist and complications that arise as personalities try to arrive at mutually satisfactory conclusions. But, on the whole, people usually prefer working with other people to working alone.

One disadvantage of working in a group is the time output. Working in a group usually takes more time to complete a task or reach a decision than working as an individual. One person will usually be able to come to a decision in less time than it takes a group of people to come to a decision. After all, with one individual there is only one mind to make up. With several people, not only does each person have to come to a decision, but then a collective decision must be made. This requires the sharing of opinions and a way of coming to a decision that will fulfill the needs of all involved. Obviously this decision process will take more time than an individual would take. This characteristic can easily be checked out the next time you and a group of friends are trying to decide where to go to dinner, what movie to see or what to do on Saturday night. Even though a group requires a longer time span to accomplish its goal, the other advantages of (1) being more accurate, (2) recalling more information, (3) increasing decision commitment, and (4) being more socially rewarding, tend to outweigh the time factor. Working in groups gives us interaction with others that is generally more beneficial than working alone.

Now that you know what small groups are, and their significance in our society, it is time to look at those rules that make all groups work.

Rules that Make Groups Work

Whether you call it cooperation or **cohesiveness**, *group members must "stick together" and work for the common good of the group.* Effective groups are made up of people who work together to solve a problem. All members give and take, equally sharing responsibilities in the group. Cooperating leads to better communication, which leads to more productivity, which generally promotes a higher morale and feelings of group loyalty. This feeling of "oneness" with the group is probably the single most important factor in making a group work. When individuals put their needs or desires above the group's needs, trouble sets into the group process.

Another important factor in making a group work is the willingness of its members to gather and share information. While there are times when group members may be assigned specific research topics, it is usually the responsibility of all group members to research the task or topic at hand. Here are some guides to gathering information:

1. Try to get the facts before making a decision on the topic at hand. Open-mindedness will allow you to keep predetermined attitudes from influencing your research.

2. Investigate several sources of information. Some duplication of data will obviously occur, but the more sources you investigate the more outlooks or approaches you will find.

3. Take notes or photocopy any pertinent information. If the information is central to the topic your group is researching or would be useful to other group members, then making copies for each person in the group may be useful.

By researching and preparing for group meetings you will make the meeting more likely to be productive. When group members fail to investigate, or only a few members research, the session is much more apt to be time-wasting or become a lecture period rather than a group working together.

No matter how much information has been gathered, it will not be of any value unless that information is shared with the group. Sharing information requires several communication skills. By keeping the following in mind you will increase the probability of getting your message across.

1. Present your information in a logical, easy-to-follow manner. If your fellow group members can't follow what you are saying, your research will have been of little use.

2. Choose terms that are understandable, clear and nondefense-producing. Define any technical words or phrases.

3. Animate your presentation with appropriate nonverbals such as facial expressions and gestures.

4. Encourage questions from your group members. This will not only foster intragroup communication, but provide feedback to you to check if your message is getting across.

5. Use effective listening skills. Listening to what others say is just as important as speaking.

Now, let's look at the organization of the group. What people make up a small group?

Leadership

The first thing which is likely to come to mind is "Who's in charge?" If this group is organized for a goal other than social interaction, which person is the one to get things going? Even though your group may not have been assigned a leader by your professor or boss, one will nevertheless emerge. With several personality types present, one will dominate and become the driving force for the group. So, you will have a leader.

What should this person be like? What are the attributes of a good leader? First of all, he/she should be confident of self, able to accept other's ideas, open-minded, generous of spirit and courteous. These sound like we are creating a paragon—an impossibly perfect person—but you'd be surprised how many people you contact who can meet these criteria.

In addition to being confident of self, the leader should be able to draw out other members of the group to determine what their thinking is on the issue. A person who is afraid of facing other and opposite opinions will not function as a good leader for the group.

What happens if your leader was chosen before the groups assembled and when you got together, this person was simply not up to the task? What can you do? *Change leaders!* Your group is a democratic organization, and as such is ruled by the same rules that exist in our society—majority rules. This implies that when enough of the group members feel that a change at the top is in order, that change should take place. Remember, we are functioning as a group, not as individuals, and the group's goal is more important than any one individual's search for ego gratification. Occasionally, your group may be saddled with a real dud of a chairperson. If this is the case, try every way possible to remove this person from that position of leadership, or your work in the committee or group is doomed. With the proper chairperson, however, your group stands a good chance of reaching whatever goals have been set for it and doing so with a minimum of hassle all around.

Remember that a leader will emerge whether one is appointed or not. Furthermore, an effective leader facilitates the achievements and tasks of the group; he or she does not assume responsibility for doing everything.

Individual Roles

Just as the leader has a role to play, so do the individual members of the group. Those roles fall into three general categories: task roles, maintenance roles and personal roles. As we describe what is involved in these areas, we are sure you will be able to recognize your friends and perhaps yourself as having fulfilled these roles in small groups.

Task roles involve the actual business of the committee. These would be people who plan the place for the meeting, the person who acts as recorder or secretary, the person who tries to investigate each person's opinion on the topic, one who drives the committee to its goal—energizes it. These are the task-oriented roles within the committee or group.

The **maintenance roles** have to do with development of group cohesion. Similar to the task roles, these roles allow the group to interact in a smooth and supportive way for the good of the group. These roles are such things as compromiser, encourager and harmonizer. Such maintenance roles are most useful in reaching the goals set for the group.

Unfortunately, since groups are composed of human beings, we will have those who will have **personal roles**—those who believe they are more important than the group as a whole. It is these personal roles which bring frustration to group work. You will have no trouble recognizing them. These are such roles as the aggressor, the playboy/girl, the help seeker, the blocker and the special-interest pleader. These few examples show you the selfish characteristics of these personal roles and their disregard for the larger goal of the committee.

Now that we have investigated the roles played within the group, let's look at the variety of group experience which you may face. As we discuss these we shall make suggestions for group projects in your individual classes.

Various Types of Small Group Experience

Round-table Discussion. These groups are good to set up when you wish to gather a large amount of information on a controversial topic, but do not wish to come to any definite plan of action or behavior as a result of your discussion. Here you might take a topic like "endangered species" and each of the panel take one country or animal to research and bring back the information which is then shared with the group. This also might be the brainstorming session to begin the investigation of a large topic. As each member presents his/her observation on endangered species, the group begins to see where more information would prove useful in discussing and understanding the problem.

Debate. Although this formal forensic activity is not as popular now as in the past, it is a good way to present information, both affirmative and negative, about an issue. As each side presents its argument, the listeners try to pick holes in their arguments by producing contradicting evidence or using logic. Usually the teams are composed of two members each, to be given an initial presentation of 10 minutes, and a rebuttal time of 5 minutes for a total time of one hour.

Problem-solving Groups. These group tasks are to go out from the larger class, and in groups of five to seven people, gather information on a social or political issue currently in the public forum. Having gathered the information, the group meets before the presentation to the class and decides upon a plan of action to meet the problems they have researched. For example, if the group takes the issue of "censorship," each member researches a given area of censorship: books, movies, videos, music lyrics, public speeches, etc. When they meet again after their research, they each present their given knowledge, and come up with a plan which might address the problems they read about regarding censorship.

From the above paragraphs you can see that the opportunities in small groups are large, and we have limited our discussion to the classroom setting here. By now we feel that you are able to expand your thinking about small groups and to apply what we have given here to the individual situations as you find them in your job or community organizations.

Parliamentary Procedure

As early as the thirteenth century with the signing of the Magna Carta, small groups began to take and control political power. With the rise of representative democracy in England certain individuals were chosen to carry out the will of the majority regarding certain governmental practices. In order to accomplish this goal, specific rules of procedure have evolved. You may have encountered these rules in the organizational pattern of some of the clubs you have been a member of. These rules of procedure, which bear the name of the English representative body, Parliament, are based upon democratic principles which allow all members of the group to state their opinions in an orderly fashion leading to a thorough discussion of the issue at hand and, hopefully, a reasonable decision reached by the majority of those representatives present. It is upon this foundation that the framers of our Constitution based the legislative body of our nation. **Parliamentary procedure** is simple and efficient, based as it is upon a standard format for an agenda (the order in which issues are discussed), and a set of guidelines for accomplishing the business at hand. This is the method employed by our legislatures on the state and national levels, and is also employed by most civic, fraternal and religious groups regardless of size. (For a concise coverage of this topic see *The Practical Guide to Parliamentary Procedure*, Second Edition, by Edward Strother and David Shepard, published by Tichenor Publishing Company, Bloomington, Indiana).

When the term parliamentary procedure is mentioned, many students get a picture of some stuffy chamber where people are jumping to their feet screaming phrases like "Point of order!" "Mr. Chairman, I had the floor!" or "Madame Chairman, I move to adjourn!" There would appear to be little organization here. But let's offer another scenario. Your group has assembled. The chairperson is at the podium. Following the basic agenda which follows, the first thing that happens is the chairperson calls for the meeting to begin: the "call to order." Assuming the group has met before and has selected a secretary to record the actions of the assembled body, we then have the reading of those actions called the "minutes of the previous meeting." After the secretary has read the minutes, the chairperson will state: "If there are no additions or corrections, the minutes will stand approved as read." The meeting then proceeds through each section of the agenda, pausing as need be, for questions or motions from the floor concerning the topics brought up before the group. Each meeting is different. Sometimes emotional issues are presented and discussed heatedly. But order can be maintained and business can be accomplished when members respect each other's rights to be heard and maintain relevancy.

Sample Agenda

The standard form for the agenda is as follows:

1. Call to order
2. Reading of the minutes of the previous meeting
3. Treasurer's report
4. Reports from committees
5. Old business (any topic previously discussed by the group)
6. New business
7. Announcements
8. Adjournment

Motions

The business accomplished during the use of parliamentary procedure takes the form of **motions** which are statements by any member of the group, after recognition by the chairperson, of action that member would like taken by the group. The proper words for introduction of a motion are "I move . . ." *never*, "I make a motion"!

The steps for a passage of a motion are as follows:

1. Motion is made.
2. Motion is seconded. (Another member says it ought to be done.)
3. Discussion is held. (Here both sides of the issue are investigated, amendments are perhaps added here.)
4. Vote is taken.
5. Results of the vote are announced by the chairperson.

Here it might be appropriate to elaborate on the role of the chairperson. He or she must keep the goals of the organization in focus, free from his or her individual bias. It is not an easy role to play, but with experience and sound judgement the chairperson can lead the group to significant accomplishments through mutual effort and understanding.

Now, we offer a word about the recordkeeper, the secretary. This is the person whose responsibility it is to keep an accurate on-going record of the business being discussed (see Appendix B for an example of minutes). He or she will not be able to remember everything, so careful note-taking skills are essential. The person designated as secretary may feel it necessary to tape the proceedings and base the written minutes on that audio tape. It is part of the organizing plan of parliamentary procedure to have an accurate record of the proceedings. For a "hands-on" experience with parliamentary procedure your instructor may wish to employ the following exercise.

Panel Discussion

Purpose: This exercise will give the student experience in working in groups aimed toward a goal. As the discussions are presented, the class can be turned into a meeting run by parliamentary procedure.

Procedure: Split the class into groups of three to five persons. A leader may be designated or decided by the group. Have the groups assemble and choose a topic of local, state, national or international interest (a local tax proposal, building renovations, abortion laws, foreign aid, terrorists, etc.). Allow the groups to go out and gather information on the topic, choosing a specific area for each person to cover. For example, if the topic is abortion, one person might take the subject of sterilization procedures; another might cover the psychology of the woman involved in an abortion. Each person will be responsible for a five-minute talk on his or her topic. The chairperson of the group will introduce the topic, define terms and, at the end of the presentation, propose a motion for action of the class as a whole. When the proposal (motion) is seconded and discussion begins, the entire class may ask questions to clarify the issues discussed. The motion is then voted upon and the results announced. (See the steps for passage of a motion above.) Assign some member of the class, who is not on the panel, to take minutes of the meeting and discussion which will be read at the following class meeting. (See Appendix B for minutes to a meeting.)

As far as what role the individual group member plays in the parliamentary procedure is concerned, we suggest that if your participation in small groups helped to reach an equitable and educated decision, so too your participation is necessary in the larger group. Remember, the majority rules in parliamentary procedure. You may not be able to sway enough of the large group to vote your way, but at least you have the opportunity to state your feelings on the topic. Get your ideas out there on the table. Let the group know how you feel. Then, no matter what the final outcome or vote, you have expressed your opinion.

Conclusion

After reading about the benefits, problems and roles required in group decisions, you may have come to the conclusion that working in groups is too complicated. You may be thinking that it's easier to work as an individual and avoid group situations altogether. This is unnecessary and impractical. Unless you are planning to become a hermit in the mountains of Colorado or on the craggy shores of New England, you will need to function in at least informal group situations. Secondly, whether you are aware of it or not, all these factors are at work in all groups whose meetings you currently attend. Knowing these principles may help you work effectively in your groups to meet the goals established.

Study Questions

1. Why are groups organized?
2. Name three groups of which you are a member and the roles you perform in each.
3. Name one advantage of using parliamentary procedure.
4. List the five steps in passing a motion.
5. Discuss the benefits of working in a group.
6. Discuss roles that aid the group's accomplishments, and those that hinder them.

Key Words

Cohesiveness	Personal roles
Debate	Problem-solving groups
Maintenance roles	Round-table discussion
Motions	Small group
Parliamentary procedure	Task roles

Appendix A

Sample Syllabus
16-Week

Week one: Get acquainted. Introduce self or another class member.

Week two: Cover Chapter I—Assign "Icebreaker" speech.

Week three: Cover Chapter II.

Week four: "Icebreaker" presentation.*

Week five: Cover Chapter III. Assign "Research" speech. (This is a five- to seven-minute speech to inform with a formal outline and a bibliography which includes five sources outside the speaker's mind.)

Week six: "Research" speech presentation.

Week seven: Cover Chapter V. Assign "Reading" speech. (This is a three- to four-minute selection of prose, poetry or a children's story emphasizing diction and vocal variety.)

Weeks eight and nine: Quiz I. "Reading" presentation.

Week ten: Cover Chapter VII—Small Groups. Set up panels and do research. (See Panel Discussion exercise.)

Week eleven: Research.

Week twelve: Small group presentation and parliamentary procedure.

Week thirteen: Assign "Persuasion" speech. Cover Chapter VI.

Week fourteen: "Persuasion" speech presentation. Assign Final speech. (This is an eight- to ten-minute speech to inform, entertain or persuade with formal outline.)

Weeks fifteen and sixteen: Quiz II and "Final" speech presentation.

*Depending upon the size of the class, presentations may take a week or longer. A class of 25 will complete a 5-minute presentation assignment in three 50-minute class periods with some time for comments after each day's speeches.

Sample Syllabus
10-Week

Week one: Get acquainted. Introduce self or another member of class. Chapter I.

Week two: Assign "Icebreaker Speech." Cover Chapter II.

Week three: "Icebreaker" presentation.* Assign "Research Speech." (The Research Speech has an outline and bibliography containing at least five sources outside the speaker's mind.) Cover Chapter III.

Week four: "Research" presentation and cover Chapter V. Assign "Reading Speech." This speech is a three- to five-minute presentation of prose, poetry or a children's story emphasizing diction and vocal variety.

Week five: Quiz I. Cover Chapter VII. Set up panels (see Panel Discussion Exercise).

Week six: Panel presentations and parliamentary procedure.

Week seven: Chapter VI. Assign "Persuasion Speech."

Week eight: Quiz II. Cover Chapter IV. Assign "Final Speech." The final speech is an eight- to ten-minute speech to inform, entertain or persuade.

Weeks nine and ten: Final presentations.

---

*Depending upon the size of the class, presentations may take a week or longer. A class of 25 will complete a three- to five-minute presentation assignment in three 50-minute class periods with some time for comments after each day's speeches.

Appendix B

Sample Agenda

The standard form for the agenda is as follows:

1. Call to order.
2. Reading of the minutes of the previous meeting.
3. Treasurer's report.
4. Reports from committees.
5. Old business (any topic previously discussed by the group).
6. New business.
7. Announcements.
8. Adjournment.

Sample Minutes

Panel Discussion I
March 29, 1993

Call to Order: 9:30 A.M.

Roll Call: Susan Black, Chairperson
Tom Dean
Julie Bequette

Committee Report: Space Exploration/The Final Frontier?

A report was given by the panel mentioned above on the past, present and future of the United States Space Program. Americans spend more money on cigarettes, liquor and travel than the government spends on the entire Space Program.

Our society has been affected by the advances made in the Space Program. For instance, modern space suits were designed to be lightweight and waterproof; thus, giving someone the idea to make a disposable diaper to keep wetness away from the baby. Also, space suits were flame retardant, giving yet another individual the inspiration to create children's clothing and blankets that are flame retardant.

Some other advancements not discussed in great detail were:

Communication satellites—help reduce cost for long distance phone calls.

Medicine

Weather

"The accomplishments of the Space Program must be evaluated in decades, not by cost."

We were left with one final thought, "What is our future in Space?"

Proposal:	A motion and second that there be a special section on the Federal Income Tax Form to give individuals the opportunity to donate to the Space Program. Carried.
Announcements:	There will be another Panel Discussion on Thursday, March 31, 1988.
Adjournment:	10:20 A.M.

Appendix C

Sample Speech Evaluation Form

Speaker   Grade

Topic

Speech No.

    I. Delivery
       A. Eye Contact
       B. Posture
       C. Gestures
       D. Facial Expression
       E. Grammar
       F. Pronunciation
       G. Enunciation
       H. Vocal Variety
       I. Attitude towards Audience and Subject

   II. Content
       A. Topic Choice
       B. Organization
       C. Supporting Material and Bibliography
       D. Introduction
       E. Conclusion

  III. Overall Impression:

Glossary

Ad misericordiam   A process of argument which ignores the issues and appeals to the sympathy of the audience. Example: A man applying for a job ignores a boss's question about his qualifications, and begins to tell the boss instead about his crippled wife and five children.

Adrenalin   A hormone produced by the body under stress resulting in superhuman strength.

Appearance   The speaker's nonverbal presentation at the podium— includes hairstyle, clothes, facial expressions and posture.

Audience analysis   The process which involves gathering demographics about your listeners, such as age, sex, occupation, etc. and applying it to insure their interest in your speech.

Audio   Of or pertaining to sound. Example: The "audio-receiver" is that mechanism which picks up sound waves.

Audio/Visual aids   Such devices as posters, pictures, charts and recordings that are used by the speaker to aid in getting his speech across to the audience.

Bibliography   A list of sources in alphabetical order.

Brainstorming   An uncritical process for stimulating thinking on a topic.

Communication   A free exchange of thoughts, feelings and ideas.

Conclusion   The last segment of the speech which gives the audience a kernel of the speech to ponder in the future.

Content   Subject material presented in a speech.

Contradictory premises   An instance in which the first half of the sentence disclaims the second half. Example: "If God can do anything, can He make a stone so heavy He can't lift it?"

Decoding   Translating verbal or nonverbal symbols into mental

169

images. Example: My mother says, "Get the hammer." I "decode" her words and visualize that specific tool she needs.

Delivery   The process of presenting your information to an audience.

Demographics   Data concerning a group of people (an audience): age, interests, income, etc., used in audience analysis.

Diaphragm   A thin, rubber-like membrane which stretches under your lungs from your solar plexus to your spine and which controls the amount of air your lungs can inhale.

Dicto simpliciter   Unqualified generalization (a logical fallacy). Example: Exercise is good for you. Therefore, all people should exercise.

Encoding   Translating mental images into symbols. Example: I wish to ask a girl to go to the theater with me. I visualize the actual place, and when I see her, I ask her. I turn my mental image of us sitting in the theater into a request for her to join me on Friday night at the theater.

Entertaining speech   That speech form whose main purpose is the amusement of an audience.

Environment   The total experience pattern, background and value scheme that a person speaks from.

Ethics   A system of morals or code of behavior.

Eulogy   That speech which is given at funerals and which celebrates the life of the deceased.

Extemporaneous speech   That kind of speech prepared from an outline, prepared until certain patterns of the ideas become fixed, but is not memorized or read from a manuscript.

Eye contact   Facing and meeting the audience's eyes with your own.

False analogy   A comparison in which the elements compared are too dissimilar to be effective in the persuasion. Example: "Our country is like a large ship."

Feedback   The verbal and/or nonverbal message the receiver sends the sender verifying the message.

Focusing   The process of determining the specific idea for the speech.

Gestures   The speaker's use of his or her hands and arms to add emphasis to important points in the speech.

Hasty generalization   A conclusion reached from too few instances. Example: You don't speak French. I don't speak French. Therefore, I must conclude that no one at our school speaks French.

Hearing   The reverberation of sound waves on the ear.

Hidden agenda   A purpose for an audience gathering which is not specifically stated. P.T.A.'s meet to discuss problems in the classroom, but they also develop a rapport between faculty and parents.

Hypothesis contrary to fact   That statement which assumes something that is not fact. Example: "If Jimmy Carter had won the last election . . ."

Impromptu speech   A speech given on the spur of the moment without any formal preparation.

Inertia   The tendency exhibited by most people to avoid change.

Informative speech   That speech form whose main purpose is the giving of facts.

Introduction   The first section of a public speech which presents the topic, gains attention and connects the speaker to the audience.

Larynx   The "box-like" structure located at the top of the trachea which produces vocal sound by means of air from the lungs just below.

Listening   An active willingness of a receiver to hear and understand a speaker.

Logic   The orderly succession of details leading to an understandable conclusion.

Manuscript speech   A speech prepared and written word-for-word, limiting spontaneity and versatility on the part of the speaker during delivery.

Memorized speech   A manuscript speech prepared word-for-word which has been committed to memory.

Model   A pictorial representation of an idea or concept.

Mood   The created atmosphere or feeling of a selection or speech.

Needs   The desires which motivate choices in human beings and which are the basis of the persuasion speech.

Noise   Physical or psychological barriers to the accurate sending or receiving of a message. Example: I find it hard to carry on a conversation in a bar with a loud band (physical noise). Because I am an alcoholic, I cannot hear your message about alcoholism (psychological noise).

Nonverbals   Those elements of the communication which are not specific language: eye contact, gestures, tone of voice, etc.

Parliamentary procedure   An organized, democratic routine to allow a large group to accomplish business.

Pharynx   The throat.

Pitch   The musical equivalent of vocal delivery, high or low.

Podium   The structure used to hold the speaker's notes and upon which the speaker may rest his or her hands.

Poisoning the well   Slander or personal attack on an opponent in an argument. Example: "You cannot believe a word my opponent will say. He's a liar!"

Post hoc   A phenomenon brought about by a cause different from the one stated. Example: "Let's not take Sam on the picnic with us. Every time we take him, it rains."

Rate   The speed of speech.

Receiver   The intended target for the speaker's message.

Regionalism   An expression or pronunciation which is peculiar to one area of the country. Example: The Southern "y'all" or the

Northeastern lack of "r" as in "pahk" for "park."

Research   The process of gathering information for your speech which may include quotations, statistics or examples.

Sender   The person who starts the communication process.

Semantics   The study of the meaning of words.

Small group   A collection of 3 to 13 people organized and interacting for the purpose of attaining goals identified by those members present.

Special occasion speech   A speech designed to keep the audience's attention and interest for a short period of time. Also referred to as entertaining or after-dinner speech.

Specific purpose   A simple sentence that states the response the speaker wishes the audience to have at the end of the speech.

Stage fright   The physical and psychological (often unfounded) apprehension or fear of a public performance.

Standard American Speech   That form of speech pattern viewed on television and heard on most large-area radio stations which is relatively free of regional accent or inflection.

Status quo   The existing state of affairs or conditions which the persuasion speech addresses.

Supporting material   The details and examples which explain and define the main points of the speech.

Symbol   A word or gesture or other representation, which stands for a mental image.

Tone   The combined verbal elements of presentation (rate, pitch and volume) which produce an emotional touchstone for the subject the speaker covers.

Visual aid   Pictorial or other visible element like a chart, picture, diagram or model which explains and illustrates some facet of presentation.

Volume   The degree of loudness or softness of vocal delivery.

White-knuckle Syndrome   The process of gripping the podium so tightly that the audience can see the knuckles turning white.

Index